D1178931

A gift for

Mary

from

Denise

XX

The
SISTERS'
Book

FOR THE SISTER WHO'S

Best at Everything

ALISON MALONEY

Illustrated by Katie May

Michael O'Mara Books Limited

First published in Great Britain in 2010 by
Michael O'Mara Books Limited
9 Lion Yard
Tremadoc Road
London SW4 7NQ

Copyright © Michael O'Mara Books Limited 2010

All rights reserved. No part of this publication may be reproduced, stored in a retrieval system, or transmitted by any means, without the prior permission in writing of the publisher, nor be otherwise circulated in any form of binding or cover other than that in which it is published and without a similar condition including this condition being imposed on the subsequent purchaser.

A CIP catalogue record for this book is available from the British Library.

Papers used by Michael O'Mara Books Limited are natural, recyclable products made from wood grown in sustainable forests. The manufacturing processes conform to the environmental regulations of the country of origin.

ISBN: 978-1-84317-460-8

1 3 5 7 9 10 8 6 4 2

Cover design by Angie Allison, from an original design by www.blacksheep-uk.com

Cover illustration by Robyn Neild

Designed and typeset by K DESIGN, Somerset

Interior illustrations: www.katiemay.me.uk

Printed and bound in Great Britain by Clays Ltd, St Ives plc

www.mombooks.com

For Kirsty,
a truly lovely sister

Contents

Introduction

'Sisters function as safety nets in a chaotic world simply by being there for each other.'

CAROL SALINE

She's your best friend, and occasional enemy; she's the yin to your yang. She's your rival and your biggest fan. Above all, a sister is a constant support and the person you know you can always turn to when things go wrong.

Sisters share more than a family history. They have shared bad hair days, hopeless diets, plots against Mum and Dad, silly squabbles and numerous laughs. They have cringed together in the face of embarrassing parental behaviour, fought over fabulous shoes, learned together, played together and endured the same family holidays.

This book celebrates the joy of sisterhood in all its complex glory. With the wit and wisdom of sisters – and brothers – past and present, true stories and practical tips, it examines the special bond between siblings, and advises on the potential pitfalls that can rock the boat.

A sister holds a unique position in your family. She is a relative, but also a friend. A support, but also an annoyance (at times). Perhaps most importantly, she's a lifelong companion through thick and thin.

From cradle to grave, a good sister is a constant blessing. Reliable, loyal and loving, let's hear it for you – the sister who is best at everything.

'Children of the same family, the same blood, with the same first associations and habits, have some means of enjoyment in their power, which no subsequent connections can supply.'

JANE AUSTEN, *MANSFIELD PARK*

Family Ties

> 'For there is no friend like a sister in calm or stormy weather;
> To cheer one on the tedious way,
> to fetch one if one goes astray,
> to lift one if one totters down,
> to strengthen whilst one stands.'
>
> CHRISTINA ROSSETTI

A sister is like a precious antique vase: a beautiful gift, which must be handled with care. No matter what the age gap, it is an extra-special relationship and one that will influence so many parts of your life.

An older sister is like a second mum, caring for and protecting her siblings – and occasionally telling them off, too.

A younger sister is a cute addition to the family as a child and will often look up to big sis, emulating her throughout her teens and growing into a close friend and invaluable support.

A SISTER IS A FRIEND

A sister is always there when you need someone to talk to. She's a shoulder to cry on, an ear to bend and a pal to share the good times with.

You've both come from the same background and ganged up against your parents together, so she understands you better than anyone else. She'll be the first to help you out when you're in trouble and the first person to whom you want to tell your good news.

In short, she's the best friend you could ever have.

FAMILY FEUDS?

Even so, you'd better keep her sweet!

Hell hath no fury like a sister scorned, and a feud between siblings can turn very nasty indeed. Knowledge is power. Chances are she's the one person in the world who knows *all* your secrets ...

- who you fancy, even though you shouldn't
- where you were last night when you said you were staying over at a pal's house
- how you cheated on a crucial exam
- the passwords to the social networking sites you use
- that you were the one who broke Mum's favourite glass bowl (even though you blamed it on the dog)

Be considerate, be kind and give her as much attention as you would like to receive from her.

Remember, when you have a sister on your side, you're never without a friend.

Sister Act

The history of showbiz is littered with talented siblings who discovered their talents as children, playing, acting and singing together in their living rooms and bedrooms.

Here's a whistle-stop tour through some of the world's most celebrated sisters.

FORCES' SWEETHEARTS

With more hits than The Beatles or Elvis Presley, The Andrews Sisters became the biggest act of the 1940s and made an invaluable difference to the Allied troops during the Second World War.

LaVerne, Maxene and Patty were born in Minnesota to a Greek father and Norwegian mother. Singing together from an early age, their career began to take off in the late 1930s when their song 'Bei Mir Bist Di Schön' earned them a Gold Record; they were the first female act to receive one.

During the war, the sisters travelled all over America, and to Africa and Italy, visiting army bases and hospitals and performing for the boys. They were also renowned for treating random servicemen to dinner!

After a brief split in the 1950s, they performed together until 1967, when LaVerne sadly died of cancer.

In all, The Andrews Sisters sold 100 million records, had a record-breaking 113 chart hits – including the unforgettable 'Boogie Woogie Bugle Boy' – and appeared in seventeen Hollywood films.

'The wonderful thing was that we were together for so many years. We dressed together, we slept together, we roomed together, we went shopping together and, of course, we rehearsed together. We never separated.'

MAXENE ANDREWS

BRIT BARBIES

Born in the 1920s in Bethnal Green, London, The Beverley Sisters – who were Joy Beverley and her twin sisters, Babs and Teddie – became Britain's answer to The Andrews Sisters in the fifties and sixties. Hits such as 'I Saw Mummy Kissing Santa Claus' and 'Little Drummer Boy' made them the highest paid female entertainers in the UK for over twenty years and the first British girl group to reach the US Top Ten.

After fifty years performing together, the trio entered the *Guinness Book of World Records* as the world's longest surviving vocal group without a change in line-up. Renowned for wearing exactly the same clothes (even on their wedding days), the sisters turned up in matching suits to collect their MBEs from Buckingham Palace upon their retirement in 2006.

Following in their mothers' footsteps, The Beverley Sisters' own daughters now perform together in a band known as The Foxes, which is comprised of Joy's girls, Babette and Vicky, and Teddie's daughter Sasha.

POP PRINCESS AND *X FACTOR* QUEEN

Australian beauties Kylie and Dannii Minogue were born three years apart, in 1968 and 1971, with brother Brendan in between. They tasted fame at an early age: at first, Dannii eclipsed her older sister, but in 1986, Kylie landed the role of Charlene in *Neighbours* and was catapulted to international celebrity.

While Dannii joined rival soap *Home and Away* and launched a successful pop career, she never reached the dizzy heights of her sister's success: 'The Locomotion' became Australia's biggest selling single of the 1980s and today Kylie boasts over 60 million record sales worldwide.

Dannii, however, has never resented her sister's stardom and they are devoted to each other. 'We were raised in a family of love and support,' she has said, 'and that has not changed.'

Since then, their careers have taken separate paths, with Dannii becoming a TV presenter, fashion designer and occasionally returning to the music scene, and Kylie concentrating on her music career. Dannii's career has seen an upturn in recent years with high-profile judging jobs on *Australia's Got Talent* and *The X Factor*.

'My sister taught me everything I really need to know, and she was only in sixth grade at the time.'

LINDA SUNSHINE

'The mildest, drowsiest sister has been known to turn tiger if her sibling is in trouble.'

CLARA ORTEGA

SPANISH SIRENS

Filmgoers all over the world are familiar with actress Penélope Cruz, but few will be aware of the talents of her sibling, Monica. In Monica's native Spain, however, she is a well-known actress and dancer whom big sister Penélope has described as 'much, much more beautiful than me, and so very talented'.

Both sisters studied ballet from the age of four; aged seventeen, Monica joined Joaquin Cortés's famous dance company.

Penélope swapped dance for acting, meanwhile, and leading movie roles brought her critical acclaim throughout Europe. *All About My Mother* (1999) brought her transatlantic attention and she went on to star in numerous blockbusters including *Captain Corelli's Mandolin*. In 2009, she won an Oscar for her performance in Woody Allen's *Vicky Cristina Barcelona*.

Monica has also since taken up acting, and become a national TV star. But she acknowledges there is one barrier that prevents her mirroring her sister's success. 'I don't speak English, so I cannot foresee a career in Hollywood,' she told the *Daily Mail*, through a translator, in 2009.

Away from the screen, the Cruz sisters have embarked on a joint venture in the world of fashion, designing several ranges of clothing for Mango.

Launching the 2008 collection, Penélope revealed that it was a childhood dream for both of them: 'When we were little kids, we would take magazines from my mother and we would hide in the bathroom, my sister and I, and pretend to be designers.'

SOUL SISTERS

If you're trying to make it in the music business, it doesn't hurt to have a sister in one of the most successful R 'n' B groups of all time. Solange Knowles showed a passion for writing songs, singing and dancing from a young age and big sis Beyoncé was happy to help her out.

Born five years apart, the two girls were encouraged in their musical talent throughout their childhood. Beyoncé had released her first single at fifteen and Solange had begun working on her first album, *Solo Star*, by the age of fourteen.

In 1997, Destiny's Child burst on to the music scene, quickly scoring US number ones and two Grammy Awards. To date, Destiny's Child and Beyoncé, as a solo artist, have sold over 100 million records.

Solange contributed to that success, writing songs both for the band and for the band members' solo careers. In 2003, aged sixteen, she released her debut album, which reached number twenty-three.

Coming from a close family, the pair are in constant touch and refuse to let their differing degrees of success get in the way of their friendship.

TWIN SET OF GIRLS

Mary-Kate and Ashley Olsen are an American sensation who were acting literally before they could walk.

The Californian twins were hired to play the same character in a TV series at the age of six months. The show, *Full House*, was so popular it ran until they were eight; by then, the girls had become celebrities and had built a brand around their names, setting up their first company, Dualstar, in 1993 – when they were just seven.

By the early 2000s, their names adorned a huge number of products, including clothes, books, perfumes, make-up, magazines and even dolls. Aged sixteen, they hit *Forbes* magazine's annual rich list.

Growing up in the public eye never seemed to faze the happy-go-lucky pair, but Ashley thinks their close bond is what keeps them on the straight and narrow.

'She's always there for me when I need her,' she says of her sister. 'She's my best friend; she's just my everything.'

Surprisingly, despite their resemblance to each other, the Olsens are not identical twins. They also don't believe they are all that similar.

'Me and Ashley feel like we're totally different,' claims Mary-Kate.

OTHER SHOWBIZ SISTERS

- The Cheeky Girls, Gabriela and Monica Irimia, Europop singers.
- Vanessa and Lynn Redgrave, British actresses (Vanessa's daughters, Joely and Natasha Richardson, also followed them into the 'family business').
- Andrea, Caroline and Sharon Corr who, together with their brother Jim, make up the Irish band The Corrs.
- The Nolans: Irish pop group consisting of Anne, Denise, Maureen, Linda, Bernadette and Coleen; most famous for 'I'm in the Mood for Dancing'.
- The Pointer Sisters – June, Bonnie, Anita and Ruth – US group who had hits with 'I'm So Excited', 'Slow Hand' and 'Jump (For My Love)'.

Being a Brilliant Sister is ...

- Helping her out of trouble, without grassing to Mum and Dad.
- Lending her your last tenner to buy a must-have pair of designer shoes.
- Sacrificing a night out because she is feeling down and wants your company.
- Letting her borrow your favourite outfit, even though you've only worn it a couple of times.
- Checking out her boyfriends to make sure she won't get her heart broken.
- Handing over the keys to your car when hers has broken down.
- Making soup and hot toddies when she's feeling poorly.
- Babysitting for her kids on your only day off.
- Sharing the tears and the laughter.
- Sharing the family baggage and lightening the load.

Memories of Youth

Sisters enjoy a special bond not only because of their shared blood, but also because of their shared childhood. Growing up with someone gives an insight and an intimacy to a relationship that can never be reproduced with even the closest friends.

Sisters have witnessed toddler tantrums and teenage strops, taken part in ferocious fallouts, been on the receiving end of your worst behaviour – but they've lived to tell the tale and are still on your side.

And, on the other hand, they've also seen you grow through the growing pains, taken pride in your achievements, and cherished the unique, lifelong friendship you offer each other.

CHILDISH THINGS

That bond is forged through the games, pranks and halcyon days of childhood. Cast your mind back, sister. Did you and your siblings ever try any of the following?

SECRET CODES

It was always of utmost importance that you and your sibling could communicate in secret – without your parents having a clue what you were up to (or so you thought).

Some made-up codes were probably easier to crack than an egg, but you sure had fun coming up with them.

Perhaps you used numbers to represent letters, or reversed the alphabet, or knocked on the wall between your bedrooms – whatever your cipher of choice, Operation Secret Code was a mission: possible for you and your sis.

MIDNIGHT FEASTS

Fuelled by mass readings of Enid Blyton novels, no childhood would be complete without at least an attempt at a midnight feast – even if Dad caught you on the stairs in your nightgowns and sent you straight back to bed.

The fantasy was always of cream buns and cookies, and lashings of ginger beer; the reality was whatever was left in the fridge after tea.

WHY, YOU'RE BEAUTIFUL

As fashion of sorts becomes important to little girls, their creative flair begins to blossom. Chances are, that creativity soon led to home-grown makeovers for all the family.

Let loose with Mum's make-up bag and a sibling's bare face, the possibilities were endless. Green eyeshadow? The perfect choice. Bright red lippie is a given. And don't forget the golden rule: masses and masses of blusher!

The result may not have won any style awards, but the photographs of such sessions are certainly priceless.

TAKE A BOW

As children, we have fewer inhibitions than in adulthood, and for many siblings, the chance to shine in the spotlight of Mum and Dad's undivided attention is too good to miss.

Consequently, your childhood with your sibling may have seen you stage home-grown cabaret shows, plays and poetry readings – perhaps with a sprinking of modern dance to the latest pop hits – all devised and rehearsed in your bedrooms before the grand premiere in the living room.

MAGIC IMAGINATION

And the creativity didn't stop there. No doubt you and your sister spent hours playing made-up games too, be they complicated variations of hide-and-seek or storylines for your Sylvanian Families toys that rivalled even the most outrageous soap operas.

'If sisters were free to express how they really feel, parents would hear this: "Give me all the attention and all the toys and send Rebecca to live with Grandma."'

LINDA SUNSHINE

FAMILY TRADITIONS

As you and your sibling grew older, the family traditions that your parents established grew with you. Now, Christmas just wouldn't be the same without those family recipes, favourite baubles and annual surprises.

No one understands the importance of those childhood memories like a sister does. But the beauty of family is that they're not lost – and you and your sibling can recreate the adventures for your own children, when the time comes ...

'A sister is a little bit of childhood that can never be lost.'

MARION C. GARRETTY

Literary Ladies

Novels throughout history have tapped the rich seam of sisterhood as their central theme. The joys and tribulations of family relations provide endless fodder for the writer's pen and classic literature has thrown up many memorable sets of siblings.

Here are just a few of those classic characters.

THE BENNET SISTERS

At the beginning of Jane Austen's classic *Pride and Prejudice* (1813), Mr and Mrs Bennet, an educated man and his rather silly wife, have five daughters and a huge problem.

With no male heir, their entire inheritance will pass to a distant cousin and, unless at least one of the girls marries a rich man before Mr Bennet's death, the rest of the family will be homeless and penniless.

The novel explores how they deal with this dilemma and has fun playing with potential marriage matches for the five very different sisters.

The Bennet sisters are:

Jane – the oldest of the clan, Jane is the most beautiful, sweet and sensible. She is drawn to wealthy neighbour Mr Bingley, who seems equally taken with her.

Elizabeth – the main protagonist, and the most intelligent and witty of the five. She is initially attracted to Mr Darcy, but his rudeness and arrogance put her off; he is later drawn by her feisty nature and beauty.

Mary – the middle daughter, who is neither beautiful nor bright, although she is very bookish and attempts to improve herself through reading.

Kitty and **Lydia** – the two youngest sisters, who are as frivolous and silly as their mother. They spend much of the novel flirting with the military officers stationed in the fictional town of Meryton.

THE MARCH SISTERS

Louisa May Alcott's novel *Little Women* (1868) was based on her own life with her three sisters, Anna, Elizabeth and Abigail, and is set in the family home in Concord, Massachusetts.

The sisters in this well-loved book are:

Jo – Alcott based her main character on herself at fifteen. A tomboy with a hot temper and a passion for writing, Jo's impulsive nature gets her into frequent scrapes.

Meg – the oldest sister, who at sixteen is considered both pretty and sensible; she runs the household in their mother's absence.

Beth – Jo's favourite sister, a sweet, charitable girl who helps poor families in the local area with her mother, and who is taken gravely ill with scarlet fever in the book.

Amy – vain and spoilt, Amy often falls out with Jo. In one incident, Jo refuses to let her come to the theatre and the furious twelve-year-old finds the unfinished novel her sister has been working on and throws it on the fire. Jo tells her she will never forgive her but, the following day, the pair are reconciled when Amy falls through the ice at a frozen lake.

Each of the sisters has a prominent character flaw, which they endeavour to overcome in order to live up to their parents' expectations of how young ladies should behave. Meg is afflicted with vanity, Jo an explosive temper, Beth struggles with shyness and Amy is selfish and spoilt.

The lives of the sisters, and their children, are also chronicled in Alcott's subsequent novels *Good Wives* (1869), *Little Men* (1871) and *Jo's Boys* (1886).

THE PROZOROVA SISTERS

In Anton Chekhov's play *Three Sisters*, his lonely characters cling to each other as the only comfort in their empty lives. Written in 1900, and set in a small Russian town, the play follows Olga, an unmarried schoolteacher who longs to be wed, Masha, who is married to a nervy schoolteacher, but is hopelessly in love with an army colonel, and Irina, who has two suitors she doesn't care for.

Thoroughly miserable with their day-to-day existence, the trio dream of a new life in Moscow and amuse themselves in the meantime by entertaining the soldiers stationed in the town.

Their lives go from bad to worse when their brother marries the vile Natasha, who slowly takes over their family home and destroys their one remaining haven.

AUNT SPIKER AND AUNT SPONGE

Created by legendary author Roald Dahl in his tale *James and the Giant Peach* (1961), Aunt Spiker and Aunt Sponge are the vilest sisters in modern literature.

One tall and thin, the other greedy and round, they take in orphan nephew James after his parents die – and set about making his life hell. Their biggest sin is that they deny him the traditional escapes of boyhood, in that he is not allowed any toys or playmates.

When a mysterious old man gives James a bag of glowing green seeds, which turn an ordinary peach into a huge globe filled with talking insects, James escapes from his cruel aunts and goes on an adventure.

Aunt Spiker and Aunt Sponge were played brilliantly by Joanna Lumley and Miriam Margoyles in the 1996 film version of *James and the Giant Peach*.

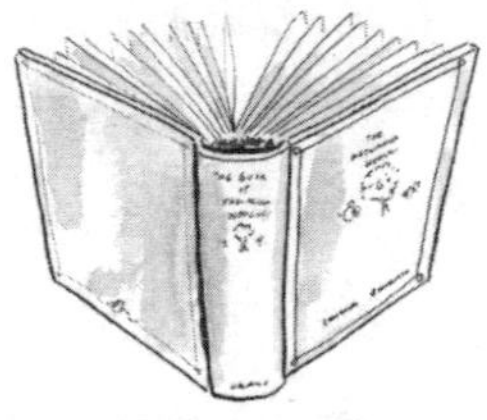

'Sisterly love is, of all sentiments, the most abstract. Nature does not grant it any functions.'

UGO BETTI

THE SCHLEGEL SISTERS

Set in the early 1900s, E. M. Forster's acclaimed novel *Howards End* (1910) is as much about the relationship between the classes as between the sisters.

The Schlegel sisters, Margaret and Helen, are frequent visitors to Howards End, a beautiful house owned by Ruth Wilcox.

In the story that follows, the sisters are nearly torn apart by their very different choice of partners, and the views each holds. But when a romantic affair leads to tragedy, the sisters once more turn to each other for support.

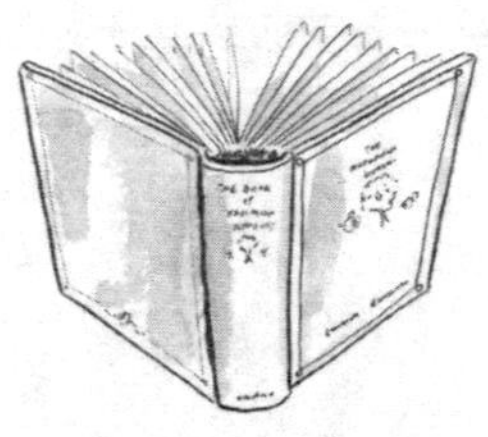

'To the outside world, we all grow old. But not to brothers and sisters. We know each other as we always were. We know each other's hearts. We share private family jokes. We remember family feuds and secrets, family griefs and joys. We live outside the touch of time.'

CLARA ORTEGA

Oh, Brother!

True tales from the complex world of brother–sister relationships ...

DISAPPOINTMENT

When Kevin's mum told him he would soon have a little sister, he was very excited.

The delighted three-year-old watched her growing bump and imagined having a little sibling with whom he could play football and pirates.

When the day came, and his new sibling arrived, he could hardly wait to meet his new playmate.

Returning from the hospital, Mum and Dad walked through the door, proudly displaying little Sally, who was wrapped in a blanket.

Kevin took one look at the tiny bundle, wrinkled his nose in disdain, and announced, 'You can take that blooming thing back where it came from!'

> 'Our brothers and sisters are there with us from the dawn of our personal stories to the inevitable dusk.'
>
> SUSAN SCARF MERRELL

SALAD DAYS

Like many siblings, Martin always blamed his little sister for everything, even though she was still tiny.

He was caught out by his penchant for salad dressing. One day, having smothered his lunch in the stuff to a ridiculous degree, he claimed, 'Ali climbed out of her cot, poured sauce all over my lunch, then got back in the cot and went back to sleep.'

Ali was fourteen months old at the time.

NO BALL GAMES

As the eldest in the family, nine-year-old Barbara knew who was boss when it came to her and her five-year-old brother, Andrew. Asserting her authority one day, she kicked him in the crotch; he ended up having to have an operation.

Barbara's explanation to her consternated parents? 'He tripped over my leg and fell on my foot.'

PARTNERS IN CRIME

Charlotte was in a panic one evening when she realized that she hadn't written a poem for a compulsory creative-writing competition, and the ditty was due in at school the very next day.

Noticing her distress, her older brother Rich asked her what the matter was. When she explained, he chuckled and then offered her the answer to her prayers.

'Do what I did,' he said. 'Take one of Dad's poems' – their father was a critically acclaimed, if relatively unknown, poet – 'and submit it as your own.'

Charlotte did just that. The poem came fourth.

'Brothers and sisters are as close as hands and feet.'

VIETNAMESE PROVERB

DINNER DISASTER

At sixteen, Kirsty was excited to be throwing her first real dinner party and had invited her boyfriend and two friends over on Saturday night. Her mum and dad were heading out and the only downside was that she had to look after her younger brother and sister.

She had planned the menu and spent all day preparing a three-course meal to impress her guests, including a beautiful pot of honeyed pork casserole.

Happy everything was under control, Kirsty went upstairs to get herself showered and dressed. As she pampered herself in the bathroom, brother Neil came home to find a note from Mum, reading, 'Dinner is in the oven,' so he found what he was looking for and heartily tucked in.

Twenty minutes before her guests were due, little sister also came home and asked Neil what was for dinner.

'I had honeyed pork,' he said with a satisfied grin, 'but there's only a tiny bit left.'

At this point, a piercing scream erupted from the upstairs landing that could be heard in the next county.

EMERGENCY OP

Siblings are always jealous of what one has that the other doesn't. When, one Christmas, Rachel's big brother John received a woodwork bench, complete with a vice and miniature saws and drills, her Barbie doll paled into nothing.

John, of course, was keen to use his new gift. Spotting Rachel's obsession, he persuaded her that the only way she might get her own bench is if they jointly put his to good use. What better way of doing that than performing an emergency leg amputation on her brand new doll?

Well, Rachel followed his words of wisdom to the letter – and was very upset afterwards when she realized that, not only did she not have a woodwork bench, but her doll was also ruined!

'I don't believe an accident of birth makes people sisters or brothers. It makes them siblings, gives them mutuality of parentage. Sisterhood and brotherhood is a condition people have to work at.'

MAYA ANGELOU

RECORD-BREAKER?

Like all big sisters, Susan knew just how to manipulate her little brother. Whenever she wanted him to do something for her, she would offer to count while he attempted to beat his previous record.

'Can you pop down the shop,' she would say, 'get me some sweets and see if you can beat your record of 52 seconds?'

Off James would go, as fast as his little legs would carry him, while Susan stayed glued to the telly.

It wasn't until James was fifteen that he realized she stopped counting as he left the house and only took up again after hearing him come in the front door.

DOUBLE YELLOW

Lucy's older brother David vowed to teach her how to drive. As soon as she turned seventeen, the lessons began.

While she was just about competent on the roads, teaching her how to park was another matter entirely. Within weeks, the car looked as though it had been attacked by vandals, it had so many dings and scrapes along its side.

David, ever keen to encourage his sis, christened her fledgling skills 'parking by ear' – when the clanging stopped, the car was safely parked ...

A RIGHT ROYAL TO-DO

Growing up in the United Kingdom, Elizabeth cottoned on to a fail-safe way of boosting her pocket money. Taking charge of her brother's fiscal education, she taught him to recognize the bank notes and coins and then confidently informed him, 'If it's got your name on it, it's yours; if it doesn't, it doesn't belong to you.'

As all legal tender in the land bore the name of Queen Elizabeth II, this childhood ploy meant that her brother was forever handing over his money to sister Liz!

'Big sisters are the crab grass in the lawn of life.'

CHARLES M. SCHULZ

A Brief Sistory

Throughout history, sisters have shaped the world. Some of the most powerful, influential and remarkable sisters are remembered here – for their solidarity, for their innovation, for their courage, even for their occasional back-stabbing ... but most of all for their impact.

THE TRU'NG SISTERS

In Ho Chi Minh City, in Vietnam, a statue of two women on an elephant, brandishing swords, pays tribute to this legendary pair.

Tru'ng Trac and Tru'ng Nhi were the daughters of a Vietnamese general, raised in a rural village and schooled in the martial arts. Growing up, they often witnessed the oppression of their countrymen at the hands of the governing Chinese authorities (in 2 BC, Vietnam was conquered by China and ruled by it for the next 200 years), but it was a step too far when Tru'ng Trac's husband was executed.

The angry widow and her sister set about raising an army of women to overthrow their oppressors. Within a few months, the female warriors had captured 65 citadels and liberated Vietnam. The Tru'ng sisters reigned as joint queens for over two years.

However, in AD 43, their enemies gathered a massive army and prepared to recapture Vietnam. Legend has it that the troops arrived on the battlefield naked, causing many of the shocked women to flee. Sensing defeat, and wishing to protect their honour, the Tru'ng sisters took their own lives by drowning themselves in the Hat Giang river.

They are national heroines in Vietnam and are still revered today.

'The desire to be and have a sister is a primitive and profound one that may have everything or nothing to do with the family a woman is born to. It is a desire to know and be known by someone who shares blood and body, history and dreams.'

ELIZABETH FISHEL

ANNE AND MARY BOLEYN

The lives of these sisters, both mistresses of Henry VIII of England, were the subject of the 2008 movie *The Other Boleyn Girl*. Although Anne famously won the hand of the King, Mary was the first to become his lover, slipping into his bed while she worked as a lady-in-waiting to Catherine of Aragon.

In 1522, Anne joined her sister at court and soon caught the eye of the monarch. Unlike Mary, Anne refused to succumb while he was married. Her clever ploy had massive repercussions, as the King broke from Rome, divorced his wife, established the Church of England and married his new love.

The sisters went their separate ways, never seeing each other again after Mary married a commoner. Anne was executed in 1536.

Ironically, if Mary had been the favoured sister at the time of Henry's divorce, history may have been very different. If the rumours are to be believed, she was the first to give him the one thing he craved most – a son.

CLEOPATRA AND ARSINOE

Arsinoe was the youngest child of the Egyptian King, Ptolemy XII, and the half-sister of Cleopatra. Upon their father's death in 51 BC, Cleopatra was due to share the throne with her brother, also called Ptolemy, but was soon deposed by him, in a move that was supported by Arsinoe.

When Julius Caesar rallied the Roman army in Cleopatra's defence, Ptolemy drowned while attempting to escape and Cleopatra was restored to her throne.

Despite the Roman tradition that POWs were strangled after victory celebrations, Caesar spared Arsinoe ... but her reprieve was not to last for long.

In 41 BC, after Cleopatra met Mark Antony and became his lover, she persuaded him to rid her of the biggest threat to her rule – her sister – and Arsinoe was assassinated.

'Sisterhood is powerful.'

ROBIN MORGAN

MARY I AND ELIZABETH I

The daughters of Henry VIII had only their father, and their bitter rivalry, in common. Mary detested Elizabeth from birth.

In 1553, Mary was crowned Queen of England, and soon after married fellow Catholic King Phillip II of Spain. This prompted a revolt, known as Wyatt's Rebellion, which aimed to oust her from the throne.

Though the uprising was quashed, it made Mary suspicious of further plots and she briefly imprisoned her sister – a figurehead for such revolts – in the Tower of London. She also set about burning Protestants at the stake, killing around 280 and earning herself the nickname Bloody Mary.

Although the Spanish were calling for Elizabeth's head, Parliament refused to allow her execution. In November 1558, Mary died childless – and the sibling she had hated all her life became one of England's most popular monarchs.

THE CLAFLIN SISTERS

Society today would undoubtedly applaud the efforts of feisty sisters Victoria and Tennessee Claflin. But in their lifetime, during the nineteenth century, they gained huge opposition and a great deal of notoriety.

In 1870, Victoria and her seven-years-younger sister Tennessee became the first female brokers on Wall Street, opening Woodhull, Claflin & Company (Woodhull was Victoria's married name, although – against the social mores of the time – she had divorced her womanizing, alcoholic husband). The career move prompted cartoon images of them as sexually wanton women in the workplace and a tag, in the *New York Post*, of 'Bewitching Brokers'.

The sororal activists used their profits to fund a controversial newspaper, which espoused views on a variety of subjects including women's rights, free love, sex education, short skirts, spiritualism and even vegetarianism. Arrested and jailed, the sisters were later found not guilty of obscenity.

Victoria Woodhull was the second woman ever to address the House Judiciary Committee, after Elizabeth Cady Stanton, and, in 1872, she became the first female to run for President of the United States.

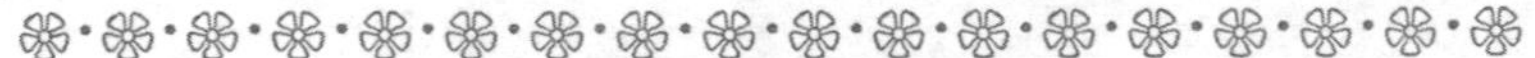

THE PANKHURST SISTERS

In 1903, Emmeline Pankhurst and her two oldest daughters, Christabel and Sylvia, set up the Women's Social and Political Union and became leading lights in the suffragette movement. The third daughter, Adela, soon followed her siblings into working for the cause.

The sisters put their all into fighting for women's votes, each getting arrested and imprisoned on several occasions. Even so, devotion to the same cause was not enough to stop the sibling squabbles and the three ended up estranged from each other and living on different continents.

Christabel and Sylvia fell out over whether the campaign should be militant or peaceful, for all women or for a privileged few; while Adela gave up the fight entirely after several spells in jail left her exhausted.

The three sisters' politicized upbringing made them passionate and ultimately influential members of society. Sadly, it also led to bitter rifts, which tore the family apart – and proved that it's never a good idea to talk politics at family gatherings!

'Two scorpions living in the same hole will get along better than two sisters in the same house.'

ARABIAN PROVERB

THE WRIGHT SISTER

Behind every great man there is a great woman, as the saying goes. In the case of the Wright brothers, it was their little sister, Katherine.

Devoted to Wilbur and Orville, she not only supported the boys financially throughout their experiments with manned flights, but also excelled at managing their business affairs.

In 1909, Katherine joined her brothers in France, where she became something of a celebrity in her own right. She persuaded the kings of Spain, France and England to watch Wilbur's demonstrations and convinced them of the safety of the new aircraft by flying alongside her siblings. She was even awarded a Légion d'honneur, a rare prize for a woman, especially in the early 1900s.

While history has largely forgotten this fascinating lady, it's entirely possible that, without her, the Wright brothers would never have got off the ground.

On 17 December 1903, Orville Wright managed to fly for 12 seconds and 120 feet – a feat now recognized as the first controlled flight in a heavier-than-air craft.

That night, Katherine received a telegram, which said: 'Success four flights Thursday morning ... Inform press. Home Christmas. Orville.'

THE MITFORD SISTERS

Born between 1904 and 1920, the Mitford sisters were an aristocratic sextet who gained notoriety in English society for their stylish, glamorous lifestyles and controversial political views, which ranged from Communism to devoted Fascism.

The Mitford sisters were:

Nancy – the oldest and most famous of the six, Nancy was the author of several successful novels, including *The Pursuit of Love* (1945) and *Love in a Cold Climate* (1949).

Pamela – briefly married to brilliant scientist Derek Jackson, she attracted some high-profile admirers, including the poet John Betjeman, but eventually became the lifelong companion of Italian equestrian Giuditta Tommasi.

Diana – perhaps the most notorious sister, she was first the lover and later the wife of the fascist leader Oswald Mosley. She and younger sister Unity attended Hitler's Nuremberg Rallies and later became friends with the Führer.

She never renounced her views, which caused frequent friction with Nancy and Jessica, who despised them.

'Sisters know one another's faults, virtues, catastrophes, mortifications, triumphs, rivalries, desires, and how long we can each hang by our hands to a bar. We have been banded together under pack codes and tribal laws.'

ROSE MACAULAY

Unity – when the family disowned Diana over her scandalous affair with Mosley, Unity rebelled and deliberately sided with her sister.

A Nazi sympathizer, in 1934 she travelled to Germany, determined to meet Hitler. In fact, she sat in his favourite restaurant every day for ten months, until he finally invited her to his table. He called her 'a perfect specimen of Aryan womanhood'; she in turn called him 'the greatest man on earth'.

Ironically, her middle name was Valkyrie, the codename chosen for a famous operation to assassinate Hitler.

Jessica – at nineteen, in 1937, she eloped to the Spanish Civil War with Winston Churchill's nephew, Esmond Romilly. Esmond was later shot down over Germany in 1941, and his wife received the news from Churchill himself, but refused to believe it for years.

Living in the US, she was a member of the American Communist Party until 1958 and wrote several books.

Deborah – the youngest of the clan, and perhaps the most conventional, she married Andrew Cavendish in 1941 and became the Duchess of Devonshire when he inherited his family title in 1950.

Together with her late husband, she has succeeded in turning Chatsworth House in Derbyshire into one of Britain's most visited stately homes.

Stages of Sisterhood

Growing up with a sister creates a unique bond which lasts a lifetime. But the easy closeness you enjoy while living together as children needs more nurturing as you grow and gain more independence from your family and parents.

Each happy milestone in her life and your own will mean that you see less of each other. College, work, moving out, marriage and children take up precious time and can put miles of distance between you. However her life differs from your own, she needs to know she has your encouragement, support and unconditional love, every step of the way.

'Sisters is probably the most competitive relationship within the family, but once the sisters are grown, it becomes the strongest relationship.'

MARGARET MEAD

COLLEGE DAYS

One or both of you opting for higher education is a strong possibility these days, and it's a huge step. It's the first time a teenager leaves the parental home and, for the majority, the first time she has to fend for herself, without the help of Mum and Dad (and her beloved sibling, of course).

REASSURANCE

After the initial joy of accepting a university place has dimmed, the nerves often kick in. Listen to her fears, and try to calm them with sensible advice. Assure her that you will always be on the end of a phone if she needs a chat, especially if it's about something she might not share with your mum or dad.

PREPARATION

Encourage her to make a list of all the things she needs to take with her, a long time in advance, and help check she has it all. Any extras she might need provide a good excuse for a girly shopping day!

Before she goes, offer to check out the area with her and look up the local nightspots, bars and cafes on the Internet. It'll show her you are interested in her new life and will help replace feelings of fear with excitement about her soon-to-be home.

SETTLING IN

The first weeks will be hardest for her, as she deals with life in a strange place, away from her family, and still finding new friends.

Spare the time to help her move in and, if she wants you to, travel up to see her for the first couple of weekends. She'll be missing the whole family, but calling Mum and Dad and asking them to come and see her might not be an option for her.

While she will want to show them that she can stand on her own two feet, she will be able to open up to you and show her true feelings. A sister is much cooler than a parent anyway – after all, who wants to drag their olds along on a cheap night out in the student bar?

AS TIME GOES ON

As she settles in and finds her feet, she may call you less, but that doesn't mean she doesn't need you. Call or email regularly to catch up or, even better, send her a funny, gossipy letter with messages from all the family and her closest friends.

Make an effort to meet her new mates, so that you can enjoy your weekends with her as much as she does.

Also remember that specialist courses at university help to develop individual passions and aptitudes, so don't forget to show a real interest in her studies. Even if she waffles on endlessly about her latest course and fabulous tutor, don't let her see you yawn!

PRACTICAL PRESENTS

The one thing that all students share is a lack of funds. When birthdays and Christmas come around, try to buy her gifts that will save her money – even if it's a boring textbook or some new socks. A basket full of toiletries, such as soap, shampoo, conditioner and her favourite make-up is also a money-saver.

If you're feeling flush, or can cadge some money from Mum, stock up her fridge with provisions. It's the one thing a student *always* appreciates.

As a special treat, bring her favourite family dish with you whenever you visit – it will make a welcome change to the obligatory beans on toast that poverty-stricken students generally live on, as well as being a wonderful reminder of home.

CAREER GIRL

After school or college, finding a job is the next big step for both of you. If you are older, your experience of the workplace will be invaluable to your sibling. Even a younger sister can lend a hand in preparation for interviews and so on.

THE HARD SELL

Help your sister put together an impressive CV, advise her on job applications and keep an eye out for relevant ads that might appeal to her ambitions.

Teach her to sell herself. One of the hardest things to do is to recognize your own best qualities, but a sister knows them off by heart. Point out the skills and character traits she should mention in applications and get her to list them, with clear reasoning as to why they would prove beneficial in particular jobs.

FIRST IMPRESSIONS

When she has some interest from an employer, help her with her interview technique. Stage fake interview panels and throw questions at her so that she can rehearse her answers. Make sure you throw her the occasional curve ball – better she is caught out by you than by a potential employer.

Give her some 'dos' and 'don'ts' to help her on her way as well. Here are a few to get you started:

Do:

- Dress smartly, even for a manual job.
- Knock before entering the room.
- Look your interviewer(s) in the eye when talking.
- Give full, articulate answers to questions, expanding where possible.
- Take a pen and pad in case you need to write anything down.

Don't:

- Chew gum.
- Slouch.
- Wear jeans or trainers.
- Swear or mumble.
- Smoke or drink alcohol before the interview.

THE RIGHT LOOK

For a first job interview, she may be lacking in suitable clothes, so offer to go shopping with her before the big day and help her choose. If money is an issue, lend her one of your own work outfits or see what you can put together from both your wardrobes.

Give her a manicure. Nice neat nails, no matter how short, look so much better than ragged, bitten ones and an eagle-eyed interviewer will be judging the smallest detail. Smart, polished shoes are also a must.

Advise her on make-up and accessories – especially piercings. A full goth look might be fine for a pint in the local, but she may need to tone it down if she's going for a job as a bank clerk.

SUPPORT AND CELEBRATE

Whatever her career choice, encourage her. You may not agree that she is taking the right route in life; while it is perfectly acceptable to suggest alternatives that you think might make her happy, you can't dictate what she does with her life. If she bags a first-class law degree, but decides she'd rather paint remote landscapes than become a barrister, that's up to her.

If her career choice takes her away from home, even to another country, try not to let your own feelings about losing her influence her decisions. Travel is relatively cheap nowadays, so think of her new home as a great place to go for a weekend away, as often as you can.

MONEY MATTERS

Inevitably, one of you will be working while the other is still in full-time education. Even when you are both employed, your wages may be vastly disparate.

In this case, be sensitive. If she can't afford to go to the expensive club in town, opt for a night in with a bag of popcorn and a DVD. Offer to take her out for a drink or buy a take-away, instead of going to a swanky restaurant. Shout her the odd cinema ticket.

As you're family, it's fine to give her money or gifts if you want to treat her. Generosity from a sibling is more acceptable, and less socially awkward than from a friend.

BRIDESMAID DUTIES

When your sister decides to tie the knot, it's time to crack open the champagne!

But, when the bubbles die down, you've got a job on your hands. Chances are you'll be picked as a bridesmaid and, without a doubt, you'll be heavily involved in the arrangements for the big event.

As a sister, you're in a privileged position – close enough to the bride to influence decisions, such as making sure the bridesmaid's dress isn't too hideous! If you're chosen as matron of honour or 'best woman', you also get to organize the hen night.

If it's your brother who's tying the knot, congratulations. Men are usually so good at leaving the arrangements to the bride-to-be that your own duties will be minimal!

BITE YOUR TONGUE

Tact and diplomacy is required on all matters matrimonial – from whether you *really* like the groom to the colour of the bridesmaids' bouquets.

Your opinion is one that your sister will value, so it's hard to avoid being asked directly. Make it a golden rule to think before you speak.

As a bride, she will be facing a daily barrage of decisions so, if you think her choice of menu is vile, or disagree with her decision to parachute into the churchyard in full wedding dress, keep it buttoned. It is her big day and whatever she says, goes.

CHOOSING YOUR DRESS

Should you be given the honour of becoming a bridesmaid, help her choose your dress, but respect her ultimate choice, even if you secretly think you're going to look like a blancmange on the day.

By now, she should know your tastes anyway, and it is fine, initially, to steer her away from colours or patterns that you know will look awful on you, but don't be too scathing about her fashion sense.

Top Tip: No matter what you have said about him in the past, do *not* insult your future brother-in-law. Whatever you think, she has chosen him as a life partner and you have to respect that.

If you have serious concerns about their relationship or know something about him that might change her mind, examine your motives before speaking out. If you feel you have to, put it as gently and diplomatically as possible and, if she still wants to marry him, forever hold your peace.

NEVER TAKE SIDES

Wedding arrangements are one of the chief causes of parents falling out with their children. Your parents will, no doubt, be over the moon about the marriage, but the run-up to the actual ceremony is stressful for all involved and when the bills start piling up, tempers can flare.

The biggest bone of contention is usually the guest list, and you may have to get used to endless rows about why Auntie Betty has to be invited but Cousin Jacob is not welcome after his disgraceful behaviour at Uncle Bernie's funeral.

Don't get involved. If your mum and sister are at each other's throats over the colour of the tablecloths, or whether the invitation should be cream or ivory (and yes, even a difference that subtle can cause friction), step away, leave the room and don't be tempted to offer an opinion. Whichever way you go, you'll upset someone!

FAMILY TRADITIONS

If she hasn't already thought of it, suggest that you provide her with an item for the traditional bridal rhyme of 'something old, something new, something borrowed, something blue'. A necklace, bracelet or even a hankie will give her something of you to take down the aisle.

A CLUCKING GOOD HEN NIGHT

It may well fall to you to give the bride-to-be a great send-off on her last night as a single girl. Sounds fun, but it comes with a great deal of responsibility, and quite a lot of headaches – and not just the hangover kind.

Step One

The first thing to do is to make a list of the guests in three categories – the must-comes, the maybes and the polite invitees.

The must-comes are the core group of friends whom she would not be without on this important night, including yourself. Find a date that every one of those can attend, as close to the wedding as possible but absolutely not the night before. (A sickly green face tends to clash with a wedding dress.)

The other two categories – those she is not too bothered about and the people she feels she has a duty to invite – can be issued with an invitation once you have sorted out the details.

Step Two

Next, decide where to go and whether there is to be a theme. Many brides now opt for a weekend away rather than one night in a club, but be aware that this can price a lot of potential party-goers out of the celebration.

If there is a theme, make it compulsory.

If there is no theme, it is a popular hen-night practice to have T-shirts printed with slogans such as 'Jen's Hen Night' or a cheekier message, like 'Kiss me, I'm the bride', if it suits her.

Here are some ideas of possible activities for the hen night:

- Hit the tourist trail – visit a big city or beauty spot and take in the sights.
- Be pop divas for the day – record your own CD or create your own pop video.
- Learn something – from burlesque dancing to cocktail mixing.

Whatever you plan, make sure it is to her taste, not yours. For example, if she is paralyzed with embarrassment at the sight of a strippergram, she won't thank you when a near-naked Tarzan swoops in and throws her over his oily shoulder.

Step Three

Don't let the hen night leave you out of pocket – be organized about the finances and make sure that the bride doesn't have to worry about a thing.

The best plan of attack on this is to give a clear indication of how much the hen night will cost in advance, and ask people to sign up to only what they can afford. Ask for money in advance of the event so that you're not chasing people for cash on the day – or even at the wedding!

> 'Whatever you do, they will love you; even if they don't love you, they are connected to you till you die. You can be boring and tedious with sisters, whereas you have to put on a good face with friends.'
>
> DEBORAH MOGGACH

Step Four

The final rule for all hen-night guests is to keep mum. Whatever happens on the hen night, stays on the hen night. It's a last blast of freedom and even if the bride did the can-can in front of the local rugby team, the groom doesn't need to know!

Most importantly, remember throughout the evening that you are in charge and you have to keep the bride safe and happy. She should not be left alone at any time and, however messy it gets, you must stay reasonably sober and act responsibly (yawn).

THE BIG DAY

On the day of the wedding, your parents will be as nervous as your sister, so you need to bring some sanity into the proceedings. Make a big fuss of the bride from the moment she gets up, and put yourself at her disposal for any last-minute panics.

In the hours while she makes herself beautiful, you may well hear frequent cries of 'I forgot my hairpins' or 'I need a cup of tea'. She may be running you ragged, but you can always get your revenge on your own wedding day.

> '[On her wedding day,] Lydia was Lydia still; untamed, unabashed, wild, noisy, and fearless. She turned from sister to sister, demanding their congratulations.'
>
> JANE AUSTEN, *PRIDE AND PREJUDICE*

A WORD OF WARNING

Unless you are 'best woman', you shouldn't have to make a speech, so relax and enjoy the big day. But go easy on the bubbly – you don't want to be hearing stories about your behaviour at the wedding for the rest of your life.

Top Tip: Keep an emergency kit of small lifesavers in your handbag. Include a small sewing kit, a nail file, lip gloss, a small packet of wet wipes, tissues, headache tablets and a packet of mints. That should see the bride through any crisis on the day.

BEING AUNTIE

The birth of a niece or nephew is the next best thing to the arrival of your own kids. If they are the first babies in the family, it is your chance to spoil them rotten, shop for those cute little baby clothes and spend hours going gaga over the new addition.

For those who already have children of their own, it's a chance to offer advice, help and reassurance to the new parents, as well as gaining a brand new addition to your babysitting circle.

For your brother or sister, it's the biggest lifestyle change they will ever experience, and you can help them out by being the greatest auntie in the world.

'I can't wait to be an auntie. It is so exciting my little sis is going to be a mum. I can't wait to get my hands on that baby bump. When the baby arrives, I am going to spoil it rotten, just like all aunties should.'

KYLIE MINOGUE

A THOUGHTFUL GIFT

The first thing you'll want to do is rush out and buy a present for your tiny relative, and who wouldn't? But stop and think first. That huge teddy bear in the toyshop on the corner looks irresistible, but wouldn't your sister prefer something more practical?

Clothes

Clothes are always a good option, but must be chosen with care. Avoid buying newborn size unless the baby is absolutely tiny or premature: most babies don't fit into them and those that do grow too big in a fortnight.

The new parents will be bombarded with 'new baby' size offerings, so it is a good idea to purchase an older age, such as 3–6 months or 6–9 months, making sure that the outfit is not too seasonal (e.g. a thick coat that won't fit until July!).

You may have to wait longer to see the baby in the clothes, but when the first round of new baby clothes is discarded, mum will be only too pleased to have the bigger sizes stashed away.

Toys

Toys that are educational may not seem appropriate when the tiny bundle has just entered the world, but it is only a matter of weeks before he or she will be reaching out to touch something colourful, or hitting a bell to make a noise.

A baby gym (if they haven't already got one) is a brilliant choice, but there are hundreds of great products on the market to stimulate little minds.

Useful Items

If your sister or sister-in-law is strapped for cash, why not make up a basket of useful items for the family – baby bath, nappies, wipes, blankets?

Throw in a few pamper goodies or a box of chocs for mum, too, and she'll be thrilled that you included her in the gift.

GIFTS FOR OLDER KIDS

As your niece or nephew grows, try to avoid filling your sibling's house with expensive plastic junk. There is an endless stream of fashionable toys advertised, which either take an age to put together and resemble a small aircraft hangar when finished, or cost more in batteries than the original price. Avoid them like the plague.

Also, steer clear of anything that makes a mind-blowing amount of noise. It may be funny to hear a voice changer, or conversation being drowned out by a toy drum, on Christmas Day, but when you've lived with it for a week or more, it's enough to cause a nervous breakdown.

OFFERING ADVICE

Your mum, and the in-laws, will no doubt be on hand to bombard the new parents with advice but, if you are a mum yourself, your sister or sister-in-law may still turn to you for certain things. Theories on baby care and raising children have changed a great deal since your own parents' day and you may be able to offer a more up-to-date point of view.

But keep your advice to the minimum. To a fraught new mum, a constant stream of 'I wouldn't do that, I would do this' can sound more like criticism than support. If she wants your input, she will ask for it.

TIME ON YOUR SIDE

You may think you have a busy life, with little time to relax, but if you haven't got kids of your own, you have more time than you realize.

Spare some for your sister. With the arrival of junior, her world has been turned upside-down and it takes a while for things to settle. She may be run ragged with lack of sleep, and sometimes have no time to herself at all, even to take a shower or do the washing-up.

A Helping Hand

It's easy to resent the fact that your sibling's attention is completely taken up with the new baby, but if you want to see her, lend her a hand. Offer to take your niece or nephew out for a walk, even if it's just for an hour, so she can sleep or enjoy a nice relaxing bath. It's the best gift a new mum can get.

Nights out may take a while to get back on track so, if possible, pop round with a tasty lunch for the pair of you, or venture out to a local cafe for a bite.

Long-Distance Auntie

Should distance be a barrier to providing everyday help, offer to visit for the weekend and help out then, but don't push it. She has just had a baby and may feel stifled already, so one more person in the house could make matters worse.

Let her know, if you are invited, that you don't expect the house to be pristine and tidy when you arrive and that you are happy to muck in with any jobs that need doing. Better still, stay with a nearby parent or relative and visit during the day.

Ladies Who Lunch

If you both have children, arrange a weekly playdate. That way you can get to have a good natter while helping each other with the babies. There are many cafes that now have soft play areas for children too, so you can gossip over a cappuccino or a sandwich while the children have the time of their lives.

Babysitting

When things have settled down at home, offer to babysit while she and her partner go out for dinner – or try to arrange girly nights out for your sis while someone else takes care of baby.

Those girly nights won't be as frequent as they used to be, but they will be more welcome than ever for that very reason.

'Siblings are the people we practise on, the people who teach us about fairness and cooperation and kindness and caring – quite often the hard way.'

PAMELA DUGDALE

THE BREAK-UP

Whether it's a short-term love or a marriage, when a relationship breaks down, a sister is a lifesaver.

It may seem a simple task – offering a shoulder to cry on and making the right soothing noises – but there are a few golden rules to remember when a heartbroken sis comes to you for comfort.

'Is solace anywhere more comforting than in the arms of a sister?'

ALICE WALKER

DROP EVERYTHING

Never make excuses in a sister's hour of need. You may have planned your own romantic dinner that night, but it can wait. Nobody's suggesting you cancel a fortnight in Barbados and rush home, but if your own plans can be rearranged, be selfless and rush to be with her. You may need her to do the same one day.

NEVER SAY 'I TOLD YOU SO'

When the bottom has fallen out of your world, the last thing you want to hear is a smug 'You should have listened to me all along'. It will only serve to make her feel more humiliated and upset.

DON'T SLAG HIM OFF

No matter how much of a rat her man has been, try to refrain from a full-blown attack on him. Express your anger at the way he has hurt your sister, of course, but don't go into a rant about his shortcomings in an 'and another thing ...' fashion.

Remember: the human heart is fickle, and by next week she may have forgiven him, taken him back ... and told him every damning word you uttered.

GIVE HER TIME

The initial fallout is one thing, and of course you are there to pick up the pieces, but don't expect her to move on too quickly.

The pain of a break-up endures long after friends and family have become sick of hearing about it, but you have the power to help by allowing her to vent whenever she wants, even if it is six months after the event. The less she has to bottle it up, the faster she'll be over it.

Long-Lost Sisters

Sadly, some sisters are separated from their siblings – by geography, by the passage of time, by adoption or by family break-ups.

Understandably, siblings often yearn to be reunited with each other. For these families, a happy ending may have been a long time coming, but it was definitely worth the wait.

COFFEE CONNECTION

A single cup of coffee brought two separated sisters together after forty years apart.

Taiwanese siblings Ho Mei-yun and Fang Chuang were two of a family of thirteen, but were given away by their poor parents in a bid to give them a better life. Later, Ho forged links with her biological family after discovering the truth; Fang, however, had no idea who her biological parents were.

By strange coincidence, both girls went to work for Cathay Life Insurance; in 2008, they travelled together to Los Angeles for a work conference. En route, Ho bought a super-sized cup of coffee, and offered to share it with Fang and another colleague.

After this, they began chatting. The subject of age came up, at which point both Ho and Fang admitted that they did not know their true birth dates as they were adopted. As they compared their stories, they began to feel a connection – and their colleague, it seems, also sensed it.

'Do you think you are separated sisters?' she asked.

Crazy as it sounded, they felt there was something in that. So, after landing at Los Angeles Airport, Ho phoned her eldest sister in Taiwan. Following a long discussion, they concluded that Fang was indeed 'sister number 8'.

Ho told Fang the good news – and the newly united siblings hugged and cried in the middle of LA Airport, while their colleagues clapped around them.

Fang later revealed that the theme of the serendipitous conference was 'Change Your Life'. Little did the company appreciate how apt that title was!

THE WONDERFUL WEB

An Internet company was the catalyst that brought Wendi Fitton and Christine Heathcote together in 2009.

The sisters had been separated by the death of their mother, Dorothy, forty-two years before. At that time, twelve-year-old Christine had been taken to live with an aunt in Blackpool, while Wendi, just three, stayed in Bolton with dad Fred.

As grown-ups, the pair had attempted to get in touch with each other, but had met with little success. Then an online tracing agency came to the rescue – and tracked Christine down through the electoral roll.

The couple had an emotional reunion over a glass of champagne in a pub near Preston in Lancashire.

'When I walked in, I knew it was Christine straight away,' Wendi later said. 'She looks like our mum – same eyes, same cheekbones. [Finding her again] was the best Christmas present ever.'

NEAR NEIGHBOURS

For several years, Ken Whitty had walked past a local lady pottering about in her garden with little interest. But in 2008, he got the shock of his life when he realized she was actually the sister he hadn't seen for forty years.

After their parents died when they were young teenagers, Yvonne and Ken had begun to see less of each other and finally lost touch in 1970. Nearly four decades later, sixty-four-year-old Ken decided to track down his sibling, placing an ad to locate her – which ultimately led to Yvonne phoning him up one afternoon.

'It happened just like that,' Ken later said. 'I couldn't believe it. I asked her where she was living and she said, "Reddish." I said, "So do I." It turned out we'd been living just 300 yards away.

'I've walked past her house lots of times and I've even seen her in the garden. We have changed so much that we just [didn't] recognize one another.'

The pair, who have four children each and sixteen grandchildren between them, immediately met up and then spent Christmas together, meeting each other's families.

'Our siblings. They resemble us just enough to make all their differences confusing, and no matter what we choose to make of this, we are cast in relation to them our whole lives long.'

SUSAN SCARF MERRELL

Superstar Siblings

Celebrities' faces are known around the world, but to some the features are so familiar they got boring a long, long time ago.

This section takes a look (and a giggle) at the sibling relationships of the rich and famous.

'My balance comes from my family. They tell me when I need to calm down, take it down a couple of notches. Then they tell me when I do something good. I think what celebrities lose is that they lose touch with reality because everybody kind of works for them. But my family doesn't care.'

BEYONCÉ

CRUISE CONTROL

Tom Cruise grew up with three sisters: Lee Anne and Marian, who are older than him, and Cass, the youngest. As a boy, he got first-hand experience of romance from Marian's pals, according to biographer Dominic Wills.

'[Cruise] remembers his sister Marian's friends ... sitting him up on the kitchen sink and using him for kissing practice,' Wills commented. 'He says the first time he almost suffocated – but it was fun.'

Tom later said: 'You started out with the older sisters' friends and then, as the years went on, it was the younger sister's friends.'

He was clearly always a heart-throb!

'I would live with all of my sisters if I could. We've always been very close, my sisters and me.'

TOM CRUISE

THE OTHER JOHANSSON SIBLING

The beautiful actress Scarlett Johansson is a twin. Three minutes after her birth, in New York on 22 November 1984, she was followed by her brother, Hunter.

She later remarked that those three minutes 'were the most important three minutes of my life'.

PAPER TIGER BURNING BRIGHT

Following the divorce of their parents, five-year-old Tatum O'Neal and four-year-old brother Griffin were left at home on their own, with disastrous consequences.

'I once used [my mother's] lighter to torch our plaid couch,' Tatum recalled in her autobiography *A Paper Life* (2004). 'It made a huge, thrilling blaze that the fire department had to extinguish, and I learned a useful lesson – to pin the blame on Griffin. He retaliated by setting my hair on fire.'

SPELL CHECK

Jake Gyllenhaal was once having lunch with big sister Maggie in New York's Wild Lily Tea Room when a stunning actress walked in. He mouthed something to Maggie and, when she didn't understand, he scribbled a note.

'Isabella Rosilini,' he wrote.

Maggie looked at the note and replied, 'No.'

'Yeah,' insisted Jake.

'No,' repeated Maggie.

'Yeah,' said Jake.

'Really?' said Maggie, and, taking Jake's pen, she corrected his spelling of the surname.

FAMILY OUTING

After interviewing Jack Nicholson for a cover story in 1974, a *Time* magazine reporter started digging around in the family background.

He soon found that John and Ethel Nicholson, whom he had been told were Jack's parents, were in fact his grandparents; their eldest daughter was the actor's real mum. After contacting Jack to ask why he had lied, the reporter was shocked to discover that the star had no idea about his genuine family tree.

'Such is the price of fame,' Jack later joked. 'People start poking around in your private life, and the next thing you know your sister is actually your mother!'

PLAYFUL PINCH

As a child, Robert Mitchum had little interest in acting, despite his sister Annette's insistence that he would be a natural. She was heavily involved in a local theatre and managed to drag him with her one night, when they happened to be casting a play.

Sitting behind him in the stalls, she waited until the director said, 'Does anyone want to play the part of ...' and then goosed him. As he shot up and said 'Ah!' the players on the stage said, 'Come on up.'

Robert did, of course, grow up to be one of the most successful leading men in Hollywood – all thanks to a very cheeky sister.

'When I was a child, I thought I saw an angel. It had wings and kinda looked like my sister.'

DENZEL WASHINGTON

Ten Things Only a Sister Would Know

- She shaves her legs with your dad's razor.
- She wet her bed until she was seven.
- She still sucks her thumb.
- If her eyebrow twitches, she's nervous.
- She sticks her tongue out when she's concentrating.
- The first time she kissed a boy.
- You once covered up for her when she was sick all over her bed.
- Her long locks are hair extensions.
- She bought her favourite designer handbag in a charity shop.
- She secretly fancies David Hasselhoff.

'More than Santa Claus, your sister knows when you've been bad and good.'

LINDA SUNSHINE

Girls' Night In

Nothing is better than chilling out with your sister. You know each other so well that there is no need for small talk or mindless chatter. If there's something to gossip about, well, it goes without saying that you'll be up all night dissecting it, but the joy of a sister is that there's no need to speak if there's nothing to say.

Make the most of your chilled-out vibe with this indulgent idea for a classic girls' night in.

SISTER CINEMA NIGHT

If you can get the house to yourselves, get together for a sister-themed evening complete with weepy movies and indulgent snacks.

Spend some time beforehand preparing favourite nibbles such as chips and dips, popcorn and mini-hotdogs. Or for something more indulgent, check out the recipes on pages 82–83 for delicious choc-dipped strawberries and oh-so-naughty caramel popcorn.

As to the main event, your movie of choice should be something sister-themed that's perfect for you and your sis to curl up on the sofa with. Why not rent some of the following suggested DVDs?

27 Dresses (2008)
Katherine Heigl is always the bridesmaid and never the bride. With twenty-seven dresses to show for her walks down the aisle, *behind* her friends, things go from bad to worse when she is invited to be a bridesmaid once more – and watch her sister marry the man she is in love with.

Great rom-com, but not a great idea if your sister is in a similar boat.

'It's hard to be responsible, adult and sensible all the time. How good it is to have a sister whose heart is as young as your own.'

PAM BROWN

Marvin's Room (1996)
Two sisters who have been estranged for seventeen years, after a row over their father's death, attempt to heal the rift when Bessie (Diane Keaton) is diagnosed with leukaemia.

Despite their differences, Lee (Meryl Streep) and her children rally round to save Bessie through bone marrow donation. Also stars Leonardo DiCaprio and Robert De Niro.

Please note: tissues required.

Margot at the Wedding (2007)
Nicole Kidman and Jennifer Jason Leigh are sisters Margot and Pauline, whose reunion for a wedding brings out their worst sides and awakens old family feuds.

Practical Magic (1998)
Sandra Bullock and Nicole Kidman star in a comedy about witch-sisters suffering through a terrible curse, which kills any man they fall in love with.

A terrific supporting cast includes Stockard Channing, Dianne Wiest and Evan Rachel Wood, and there's something for the girls in the shape of the gorgeous Goran Visnjic and Aidan Quinn.

Mermaids (1990)
A very young Winona Ryder and Christina Ricci are the children of wacky single mum Cher in this cute family comedy. The girls are constantly embarrassed by their mum's crazy antics, but the relationship is as endearing as it is unconventional.

Home for the Holidays (1995)
Holly Hunter goes through the universally recognized pain of a family celebration after deciding to spend Thanksgiving at her parents' home.

Strained relations with her humourless sister and aging parents are intensified by the mischievous antics of her gay brother, played by Robert Downey Jr, and the fact that he has brought along his boyfriend, played by Dylan McDermott.

'You keep your past by having sisters. As you get older, they're the only ones who don't get bored if you talk about your memories.'

DEBORAH MOGGACH

INDULGENT TREATS

Why not try these recipes for the perfect snacks for your girly night in?

CHOC-DIPPED STRAWBERRIES

INGREDIENTS

125g (5oz) good quality dark or milk chocolate
20 large strawberries, with stalks

METHOD

① Line a dish or baking tray with greaseproof paper.

② Break the chocolate into small pieces and place in a bowl over a pan of gently boiling water.

③ When the chocolate has fully melted, remove the pan from the heat, but leave the bowl on the pan.

④ Dip the tip of each strawberry into the melted chocolate, until it is about halfway up.

⑤ Pull out again, twirling the fruit to avoid drips, and then place the berry gently on to the lined dish.

⑥ Leave to cool and harden before serving. Tip: Keep the treats cool, but don't store in the fridge.

For extra flair, you can melt white chocolate and then drizzle over the dark.

QUICK CARAMEL POPCORN

INGREDIENTS

250g (9oz) butter
250g (9oz) caster sugar
250ml double cream
Large bag of popcorn (already popped)

METHOD

① Mix the caster sugar and butter in a saucepan and heat over a moderate hob until caramelized.

② Remove from the heat and leave to cool.

③ Slowly add the cream, whisking constantly.

④ Put the saucepan back on the heat and simmer until the cream has thickened slightly.

⑤ Leave to cool, then pour over the popcorn and serve immediately.

DRESS CODE

If you really want to make a night of it, bring your PJs, slippers and dressing gown with you and make it a proper pyjama party.

If dignity or diary dictate differently, just make sure you're wearing your comfiest sweatpants and a cosy jumper. This is not the time for designer heels and dresses – save those for the girly nights out!

Get the Party Started

Since your earliest birthday celebrations, your sibling has been on hand to get the party started. From kiddie bashes with party games and streamers to the first forays into clubbing and bars, the chances are your sister was the one with whom you painted the town red.

No matter what age you are now, that doesn't have to stop. From post-work drinks to family weddings, hen nights to big birthday dos, keep the good times rolling.

COCKTAIL HEAVEN

Nothing shouts fun sisterhood more than the idea of gossiping over an elaborately made cocktail.

Grab your best girl and take a seat at the hottest bar in town. Whether your tipple of choice is a Cosmopolitan or a Martini, savour the smooth flavour as you kick back with your sis.

If location or budget constrain your choice of venue, you could always opt for a cocktail evening hosted at home. Get dressed up to the nines in your favourite frocks, stick some piano jazz on the stereo and make your way through a cocktail book.

ALEXANDER'S SISTER COCKTAIL

You could always try this rather appropriately named beverage if you're feeling experimental.

METHOD

① Mix equal measures of gin, crème de menthe and cream with ice.

② Shake and strain into a cocktail glass.

GIRLS' NIGHT OUT

When was the last time you and your sister went dancing? Bonding on the dance floor is a really fun way to spend time with your sister.

Head for a nightspot with a fabulous glitter ball and dance the night away!

SISTER SONGS

Perhaps one of these tunes will make the night go with a sisterly swing …

- 'Dance Little Sister' – Terence Trent D'Arby
- 'Lady Marmalade' – Christina Aguilera, Lil'Kim, Pink and Mya
- 'We Are Family' – Sister Sledge
- 'Sisters Are Doing It For Themselves' – The Eurythmics with Aretha Franklin
- 'My Sister, My Friend' – Reba McEntire

'I know some sisters who only see each other on Mother's Day and some who will never speak again. But most are like my sister and me … linked by volatile love, best friends who make other best friends ever so slightly less best.'

PATRICIA VOLK

SPECIAL BIRTHDAYS

If your sibling is celebrating a landmark birthday, chances are she may be celebrating in style with a big bash.

Make sure you're at the forefront of any celebrations. Perhaps you could bake a surprise birthday cake (in the shape of the number of years she's racked up?) or volunteer to decorate the venue. Or why not lay on a bottle of champers, if you're feeling particularly generous?

For great gift ideas for special birthdays, see page 154.

PREPARATION IS EVERYTHING

Remember the fun you used to have getting ready together before a night out? Try to arrange a girly get-together in advance of the main event at one of your homes, so that you can help each other beautify yourselves, advise on jewellery and clothes, and generally enjoy that pre-night-out excitement in each other's company.

You could even fit in a shopping trip beforehand to select the perfect outfit for your big night.

> 'I know my older sister loves me because she gives me all her old clothes and has to go out and buy new ones.'
>
> ANONYMOUS

Phrases you never want to hear from your sister:

- 'Mum said you wouldn't mind.'
- 'Is it okay if I move in for a while?'
- 'It's only a few hundred quid.'
- 'My kids are always top of the class, and they came first at sports day.'
- 'You know that dress I borrowed for the party ...'
- 'You know that guy you said you really fancied ...'
- 'I thought you *knew* you were adopted!'

> 'She is your mirror, shining back at you with a world of possibilities. She is your witness, who sees you at your worst and best, and loves you anyway. She is your partner in crime, your midnight companion, someone who knows when you are smiling, even in the dark. She is your teacher, your defense attorney, your personal press agent, even your shrink. Some days, she's the reason you wish you were an only child.'
>
> BARBARA ALPERT

Bad Girls

As every sister knows, your sibling is the person most likely to become your partner in crime as you grow up. For some, it seems, that doesn't end with the passing of youth.

Here are some scandalous sisters from the archives of history – including some siblings who utterly abandoned morality to commit the ultimate crime.

BANGS FOR THE MEMORY

Born in the 1860s, the Bangs sisters were infamous Chicago mediums who made a fortune from gullible clients.

Lizzie and May Bangs were the oldest of four children born to a tinsmith and his wife, Meroe, herself a practised medium. As children, they were at the centre of family séances and apparently displayed the necessary psychic abilities to follow their mother into the business. In the presence of these 'innocent' children, messages from the afterlife came thick and fast.

By the time they reached their twenties, the sisters' fame had spread. Some of their early tricks were exposed as frauds by undercover policemen, but their popularity was unaffected and they merely moved on to more advanced trickery.

'Their elegant parlors have been crowded by day as well as by night, and money flowed into their coffers in large streams.'

THE WASHINGTON POST ON THE BANGS SISTERS, 1888

WHILE WE'RE AT IT

The inventive pair also used their 'gifts' to snare wealthy men.

May's four husbands included a wealthy chemical manufacturer, whom she met at a séance (at which she told him his dead wife and child wished him to marry her), and a millionaire leather tycoon, to whom she proposed three times, before informing him that his dear departed mother wished them to wed and had promised that the union would make him twenty-five years younger!

FOXED BY THE FOX SISTERS

The Fox sisters – Kate, Margaret and Leah – also tricked the world into believing they could talk with ghosts. But their trickery was basically a secret code blown way out of proportion. What their punters thought was the sound of a spirit and medium conversing was actually the sisters engaging in some complex knuckle-cracking.

The trio devised a systematic 'language' for the various clicks, knocks and squeaks they could create with their toes and fingers and practised their skills throughout childhood. They kept up the ruse for almost forty years, and were even declared genuine by a scientist who investigated them, one William Crookes.

They died in poverty after Margaret confessed the truth and held a toe-cracking demonstration to prove the authenticity of her revelation. She later tried to recant her admission, but the damage had been done.

MURDEROUS MAIDS

In February 1933, French lawyer Rene Lancelin arrived at his home to find the door bolted from inside and the house in darkness. He returned with several policemen, who managed to break in through a window.

Inside, they found the lights would not switch on. Using a flashlight, the police crept upstairs and found a gruesome sight. Madame Lancelin and her grown-up daughter had been beaten to death, had their fingernails pulled off and their eyes gouged out.

In the attic bedroom, they found the family maids, Christine and Lea Papin, ready to confess to the crime. The older of the two, Christine, revealed that a fuse had blown while she did the ironing, causing the lights to black out and starting a row between herself and her employer, which had led to the vicious attacks.

PARANOID DISORDER

The sisters had a reputation as good workers and churchgoers, who had no friends outside their own relationship. With the girls regularly working 12–14 hours a day, experts believe that the pair may have been victims of shared paranoid disorder, which can occur in small groups who feel cut off from the world, leading to an intense, isolated relationship.

Christine was deemed the more dominant of the two and given a harsher sentence; she died in a lunatic asylum four years after her conviction.

The murders rocked France and became something of a cause célèbre among intellectuals such as Jean-Paul Sartre and Jean Cocteau, who saw it as a class uprising.

Many articles, plays and novels have been written about the two sisters since, and there have been at least two films inspired by the events: *Les Blessures Assassines* (2000) and *Sister My Sister* (1994), the latter starring Joely Richardson and Jodhi May.

ARSENIC AND OLD LACE

Margaret Higgins and her sister Catherine Flanagan were hanged in 1884 for the murder of Thomas Higgins, Margaret's husband. But it is believed that the pair, who became known as The Black Widows of Liverpool, may have murdered many times.

Suspicion was raised by Thomas's brother, after not only Thomas but also his former wife and ten-year-old daughter had died. A post-mortem was carried out: Thomas had been killed by arsenic poisoning. As a result, the bodies of three more people who had died at Skirving Street were exhumed; post-mortems proved they had all suffered the same fate.

The motive? Life insurance had been taken out before the deaths, and the sisters had received a tidy sum from each crime. Among the victims was Catherine's own son.

Four other women were tried for the murders, but acquitted over lack of evidence. Modern historians have claimed that up to eight other women may have had a hand in the scheme and that as many as seventeen more victims may have perished.

'And lovelier things have mercy shown,
To every failing but their own,
And every woe a tear can claim,
Except an erring sister's shame.'

LORD BYRON, *THE GIAOUR*

Sibling Rivalry

'If you don't understand how a woman could both love her sister dearly and want to wring her neck at the same time, then you were probably an only child.'

LINDA SUNSHINE

As the old saying goes, 'You can choose your friends, but you can't choose your family.' You wouldn't be without her for the world but, while she's your best friend and confidante, even the best of sister relationships may have an element of sibling rivalry.

Small grievances can lead to a lifetime of petty resentments, unless the situation is managed carefully. The best way to steer your way through the minefield of sisterly relations is to recognize the flashpoints and either avoid them or learn how to tread *very* carefully.

PARENTAL CONTROL

'You were always the favourite' is a common complaint thrown at siblings, as if it were somehow their fault they got on well with their parents.

The most frequent family jealousies arise from a perceived injustice in the way mums and dads treat their respective children. Of course they don't set out to have favourites, but their offspring often get the impression that they prefer one child over another because the day-to-day relationship with each can differ wildly.

This is often down to the different behaviour and personalities of the children, rather than any preference by the parent, but it can build into a big issue in a family.

WHAT TO DO?

If this 'accusation' is levelled at you, try to reassure your sister that your parents love both of you equally, and remind her of treats and gifts that she may have received throughout your childhood.

Don't allow the conversation to become an argument, but lighten the mood. Tell her, 'You were always *my* favourite.'

Top Tip: Keep quiet about the little things that your mum and dad do for you, or that you do for them, unless she needs to know, particularly if circumstances or geography mean you get to spend more time with them.

Keep her posted, but don't brag about the lovely dinner they cooked for you last week, or a holiday you may have taken together.

GOLDEN GIRLS

When it comes to academic achievement or career success, one thing can be guaranteed – no two people are exactly the same. This may mean that your sibling is a straight-A student while you struggle to get a C, or vice versa. She may choose a high-flying career and soar to dizzy heights, while you might opt for a less ambitious route.

Unfortunately, whichever sister is perceived to be 'more successful' can also be the subject of envy.

'I get asked about Beyoncé all the time, but I try and make fun of it. Sometimes I say she's not my sister. Other times I say I've stuffed her in my suitcase and sent it to Dubai. I have to have fun with it or I'll turn into Britney – shave my head and go totally crazy.'

SOLANGE KNOWLES

WHAT TO DO?

1. Be sensitive. If your sister is younger and delighted by the B grade she just achieved in an A level, don't be tempted to remind her of your A. If you have a fabulous job, try not to brag, but remember to pay attention to the personal triumphs that she tells you about, no matter how small you may secretly think them to be. Encourage her to talk about her workplace or her daily life and show interest.

2. Accentuate the positive. If you are a high achiever in the academic stakes, praise her other talents, whatever they may be. Tell her how lucky she is that she is naturally sporty, a great artist or just able to make friends really easily. If she is a great mum, tell her you admire her parenting skills.

3. Count your own blessings. Should you feel overshadowed by a brilliant or talented sibling, remember that her life isn't perfect either. You may envy her career, but perhaps she has more stress to live with. Or you might feel a prick of jealousy over a specific achievement. Try to remember your own accomplishments and perhaps strive to add to them with a college course or evening class in something you enjoy.

4. Be proud. While parents are expected to be proud of their children, natural rivalry can sometimes get in the way of pride in our siblings. Tell your sister that you admire her and are proud of her. That's what she really wants to hear!

STYLE ISSUES

> 'If your sister is in a tearing hurry to go out and cannot catch your eye, she's wearing your best sweater.'
>
> PAM BROWN

One advantage of having a sister is that you can double the size of your wardrobe, provided you are roughly the same size. Swapping clothes for a night out means you will always have something new on hand, but borrowing each other's clothes is fraught with problems unless you follow the golden rules:

1. Never borrow without asking first. If you can't get hold of her in time, don't second-guess her reaction to you walking into the pub in her favourite dress. There could be hell to pay.
2. If she hasn't worn it yet, neither should you. She may well be saving it for a special occasion and won't be too chuffed if she's not the first person seen in the killer outfit she saved up to buy.

3. If you can't afford to replace it, don't wear it. With the best will in the world, outfits can end up ripped or stained on a night out and she won't appreciate it when you bring back her £300 designer dress with a tomato juice stain. You'd better be able to cough up for a new one in the event of such a disaster.

4. Just because it suits her, doesn't mean it suits you. Sisters come in all shapes and sizes and unless you are identical twins, you're unlikely to look fabulous in every item of clothing she chooses for herself.

5. Come clean. If anything happens to it, you need to be honest with her and make sure you rectify the problem. If an item is dry clean only, you should pay for it to be cleaned every time you wear it, and if it needs washing and ironing, don't leave it to her.

'We are the same size and we borrow each other's clothes all the time. When I stay with Penélope in LA, I borrow her clothes, and when she comes to Madrid, she takes things from my wardrobe.'

MONICA CRUZ

SISTERS AND MISTERS

The Beverley Sisters sang, in Irving Berlin's song 'Sisters', 'Lord help the sister, who comes between me and my man,' and rarely a truer word on sisterhood has been spoken.

While you may happily share a taste in clothing or interior décor, a similar taste in men can prove fatal to a relationship. Stealing a current boyfriend, flirting with an ex or dating someone she had her eye on is to cross a line that can never be erased.

These pitfalls can be avoided with these simple rules:

1. Be honest. She doesn't know you have fallen for the guy who serves at the local corner shop unless you tell her. If you both know who the other is keen on, you'll each know whom to avoid.

2. If in doubt, ask before you date. If your potential bloke has any dealings at all with your sister, even as friends, it would be wise to talk to her about it before you embark on a relationship. She may be harbouring a secret crush, or have a good reason why you should steer clear.

3. Don't flirt. No matter how well you get on with her fella, make sure your behaviour can't be misinterpreted. If you share a sense of humour or an interest with your sister's man, that's great news, but she will get miffed very quickly should that mean you spend every evening giggling with him in the corner and excluding her.

4. Hide the hate. In the opposite situation, when you simply can't stand the new guy she's brought home, try not to show your dislike. Calmly voice any genuine concerns that his behaviour may arouse, but don't slag him off. Chances are she'll react badly and feel she has to choose between you, which will be messy for everyone.

5. Don't ditch the sis. Love can make you behave out of character, so if either of you falls for a guy, make sure you still have time for each other. If you have always spent Saturday night with your sister, and you now want to spend it with him, try to compromise. Promise to go out every second Saturday or offer another day as an alternative.

   When the boot is on the other foot, be as understanding as possible, but let her know you still want her to put aside some time for you too.

'There can be no situation in life in which the conversation of my dear sister will not administer some comfort to me.'

MARY MONTAGU

CHILD PSYCHOLOGY

Nothing makes siblings more competitive than their own children.

From the moment their child is born, proud parents want to show off their offspring and tell everyone excitedly about their first steps and first words. It's hard not to boast when your little darling comes first in a music competition or top of the class in maths, but it's equally annoying for the parent whose child may not be quite as bright or talented.

WHAT TO DO?

Try to avoid comparisons between children and remember that they will develop at very different levels and paces. They all walk and talk in the end, and the one who is bottom of the maths class aged ten may still go on to be a brain surgeon or even a world leader.

Equally, try not to rise to the bait if your sister or your parents boast about the achievements of your nieces and nephews. They are your blood too, so be proud of them.

PARENTAL STRIFE

Later in life, you and your sibling will have your aging parents to care for. This can exhume the whole problem of sibling rivalry, jealousy and resentment from the past and make it very real once more.

In many families, the sibling with the most time or the least distance from their parents' home can end up putting in all the effort and being relied upon unfairly.

Equally, the sibling who is doing less can feel like they are missing out on time with their parents.

WHAT TO DO?

If you are the chief carer, make sure your sister knows that you would welcome her input, and ask her opinion about major decisions that will affect Mum or Dad's lives.

If the tables are turned, find the time to help her out, give her a break from whatever responsibilities she has taken on herself, and offer to take over whenever you can.

LADY LUCK

Whichever cards you are dealt in life, the way in which the game unfolds contains a large element of luck.

Your sister may be the kind of girl who loses a penny then finds a tenner. She may have got the thick shiny hair, while yours is unruly and knotty, or perhaps she can eat until the cows come home and stay slim, while you put on a pound at the sniff of a chocolate bar.

WHAT TO DO?

Luck can change so, should situations reverse, make sure you are there for her when she needs you, through the bad times as well as the good.

Focus on the good things that happen to you and be happy when fortune smiles on her. You never know, she may win the lottery next week – and who better to share the jackpot with than her lovely, generous sister?

Fairy-Tale Fun

Sisters have long been a feature of traditional fairy tales, just as much as evil stepmothers, fairy godmothers and those oh-so-handsome princes.

Usually, the sisters are either present as a much-needed support for their siblings, or used as a device to highlight contrasts to the heroine, such as in *Cinderella*.

Are you sitting comfortably? Then I'll begin …

THE TWO SISTERS

These two sisters were like peas in a pod, but one was good-tempered and the other bad.

Their father had no money, so the good-tempered sister decided she would find work. On the way, she helped a variety of characters. She soon became a witch's serving-maid, but the witch never paid her.

When the girl found the witch's gold, she decided to run home. Although the witch came after her, the girl begged for help from the characters she'd met before, and all protected her and she made it home safe.

The bad-tempered sister was very jealous of her sister's luck. She resolved to get her own gold – but she refused to help anyone on her way to the witch's house, and so, when she tried to escape, the witch caught up with her and gave her a good beating.

HANSEL AND GRETEL

The classic tale of a brother and sister besting their enemies.

Hansel and Gretel were abandoned in the forest after their father gave in to the cruel demands of their stepmother. Hungry, lost and afraid, they stumbled upon a cottage made from candy in the heart of the woods. At first, they thought they were saved, but the cottage belonged to a witch, who locked Hansel in a cage, intending to fatten him up before eating him!

Clever Gretel scuppered this plan when she pushed the witch into her own oven. She rescued her brother and they ran home, with the witch's treasure, to their father, where they learned their stepmother had died. The three lived happily ever after.

'Our siblings push buttons that cast us in roles we felt sure we had let go of long ago – the baby, the peacekeeper, the caretaker, the avoider … It doesn't seem to matter how much time has elapsed or how far we've travelled.'

JANE MERSKY LEDER

SNOW WHITE AND ROSE RED

Two sweet girls who found a happy ending in the same family ...

One winter, a black bear came to the door of these two sisters, requesting shelter. The girls were frightened at first, but soon the bear became their friend. They were saddened when summer came and he left.

The next time they met, they saw him kill a cantankerous dwarf with one blow. As they watched, the bear's coat fell off and revealed a handsome prince: he had been cursed by the dwarf, who had stolen his treasure, but now all was well again.

Snow White married the bear-prince, Rose Red married his brother, and they all lived happily ever after.

Sister Stories

These stories and anecdotes about sisters add a little wit and humour to the art of sisterhood.

SHOE SHOCK

Throughout her life, Jackie had had similar fashion taste to her younger sister. Unfortunately, that meant that whenever Jackie bought a new handbag or outfit, Ella rushed out to buy the same.

Finding this trait increasingly irritating, Jackie stopped telling Ella what she had bought, especially if it was something special for a family occasion.

As the wedding of a cousin approached, Jackie kept her new dress quiet and persuaded her husband, rather than her sister, to come with her to look for coordinating shoes.

Spotting a pair of designer heels, she fell in love. 'But they're £99, which is much more than I would normally spend,' she moaned.

'At least it means your sister won't be able to afford the same pair,' reasoned hubby. With that argument, how could she refuse? She raided her bank account and splashed out.

Back home that evening, she was admiring her purchase when the phone rang, and Ella was on the line.

'Guess what?' her sister gushed. 'I've found the most divine pair of shoes for the wedding. I shouldn't really have bought them, though. They were £99 …'

WE ARE VERY AMUSED

According to Prince Michael of Kent, Queen Victoria was once seated next to a deaf and rather tiresome old admiral during a dinner at Windsor Castle. He regaled her with a seemingly endless tale of a battleship that had been sunk and later towed to Portsmouth.

'The Queen, anxious to change the subject, asked him about his sister,' recounted Prince Michael in the *Daily Telegraph*. 'Mishearing her, he replied, "I am going to have her turned over, take a good look at her bottom and have it scraped."'

The Queen apparently 'put down her knife and fork, hid her face in her handkerchief and shook and heaved with laughter until the tears rolled down her face'.

POST-PARTY BLUES

When her parents and fifteen-year-old sister Karen went away for the weekend, thirteen-year-old Alex was allowed to stay behind at a friend's house. Before leaving, her mum finalized arrangements with the other mother and off they went.

But Alex and her pal had plans of their own and no sooner had the family left than they invented a sleepover at another girl's house and headed back to Alex's home, where they threw a party.

Big sister Karen was, of course, well aware of their intentions – and had a nasty surprise in store. The following morning, Karen got up before her parents had surfaced, rang her sister at home and told her, 'Quick! Tidy up! Mum and Dad have decided to come home early. We're just leaving now and we'll be back in about an hour!'

Alex took one look at the total devastation around her and made a split-second decision. There was no way they could get the place straight in an hour, so they left it exactly as it was and scarpered.

In fact, the family didn't roll up until 4 p.m. – and when they caught up with their errant daughter, they hit the roof.

Talk about party pooper!

SISTERLY SUPPORT

Three sisters, aged ninety-five, ninety-three and ninety-one, lived together in a big house.

One day, the ninety-five-year-old ran a bath and, with one foot in, yelled, 'Sisters, was I getting in or coming out?'

'Hang on,' replied the ninety-three-year-old. 'I'll see if I can help.'

Halfway up the stairs, she stopped and shouted, 'Sisters, was I going up the stairs or coming down?'

Shaking her head sadly, the ninety-one-year-old, sitting downstairs, muttered, 'I hope I never get to be that forgetful,' and knocked on the wooden table for good luck.

Then she called out, 'I'll come up and help both of you as soon as I see who's at the door!'

'Sibling relationships outlast marriages, survive the death of parents, resurface after quarrels that would sink any friendship. They flourish in a thousand incarnations of closeness and distance, warmth, loyalty and distrust.'

ERICA E. GOODE

Screen Sisters

'Do you ever hear Dad introduce us to people? "This is our daughter Dottie, and this is our other daughter, Dottie's sister."'

LORI PETTY, *A LEAGUE OF THEIR OWN*

Films from across the years have featured or focused upon sisters. Whether the movies are making the most of this potentially dramatic and explosive relationship, or simply demonstrating quietly the unique strength and support that sisters supply, here are some of the most memorable siblings from the silver screen.

Whatever Happened to Baby Jane? (1962)

Bette Davis stars as the most psychotic sister in cinematic history, former child star 'Baby Jane'. After her career fades, and older sister Blanche becomes a celebrated film star, the pair are involved in a car accident and Blanche is crippled for life.

Years later, the pair are living in a huge mansion, seeing no one between their weekly visit from the cleaning lady. In their isolation, deranged Jane keeps her crippled sister, played by

Joan Crawford, as a virtual prisoner, and thinks up ever more vicious and macabre ways to torture her.

A classic tale of sibling rivalry taken to extremes.

IN A NUTSHELL: Twisted sister.

The Color Purple (1985)

Whoopi Goldberg and Akosua Busia star as sisters struggling through life in America in the early 1900s.

At the start of the film, seventeen-year-old Celie (Goldberg) is giving birth to her second child by her own father, which is then taken from her. Forced to marry a local farmer, she is beaten and abused by him until Nettie (Busia) comes to stay, fleeing the unwelcome advances of their dad.

Nettie later leaves and tells Celie only death would stop her from keeping in touch. When no letter arrives, Celie despairs of ever seeing her sister again.

Nominated for eleven Oscars, Steven Spielberg's adaptation of Alice Walker's novel is a deeply touching story.

IN A NUTSHELL: Tissue box at the ready.

Hannah and Her Sisters (1986)

Mia Farrow, Barbara Hershey and Dianne Wiest share more than a meal in this comedy about sisterhood. Set around two Thanksgiving celebrations, perfect wife Hannah (Farrow) gets her family together, only to have her husband (Michael Caine) fall for her sister Lee (Hershey).

To add insult to injury, her other sister, Holly (Wiest), then sparks up a romance with Hannah's hypochondriac ex, played by Woody Allen, who also wrote and directed the film.

Hilarious and touching, this Oscar-winning movie is one of Allen's best.

IN A NUTSHELL: Forget love triangle; try love pentagon.

The Virgin Suicides (1999)

Five beautiful teenage daughters of a maths teacher become the subject of local gossip when the eldest commits suicide, and the family become recluses.

The neighbourhood boys are fascinated by the four remaining Lisbon sisters, who are locked away, day in and day out, as their house falls into disrepair. A year after the first suicide, the boys are invited into the family's home. Shortly after they arrive, the four sisters take their own lives.

A disturbing tale of teenage angst told from the point of view of the local observers, trying to piece together the tragedy some years later.

IN A NUTSHELL: Sisterly similarity with tragic consequences.

In Her Shoes (2005)

Toni Colette is Rose, a sensible lawyer and compulsive shopper, while Cameron Diaz is Maggie, her beautiful but sexually promiscuous little sister. After she is thrown out by her step-mother, Maggie begs a room at her sister's apartment and then repays her by bedding Rose's boyfriend.

Cast out once more, Maggie goes in search of a long-lost grandmother in an attempt to forge a new family bond.

IN A NUTSHELL: Family betrayal and forgiveness.

Rachel Getting Married (2008)

Recovering addict Kym (Anne Hathaway) turns up at the family home for the wedding of sister Rachel, and is annoyed to find she is not the maid of honour. The tensions between the siblings boil to the surface as their father's concern for his troubled daughter seems like favouritism to her jealous sister.

As the situation erupts, a family secret resurfaces and threatens to blow the family apart.

A stunning performance by Hathaway, who was nominated for an Oscar for the role, and an honest story that any sister will relate to.

IN A NUTSHELL: You can choose your friends, but you can't choose your family.

My Sister's Keeper (2009)

Abigail Breslin stars as an eleven-year-old who has been brought into the world as a genetic match for her older sister, who has leukaemia.

Subjected to various medical procedures from the age of five, she rebels when asked to donate a kidney and seeks a lawyer's help to gain emancipation from her parents.

Cameron Diaz is the obsessed mother, who aims to fight one daughter to the bitter end in order to save the other.

A powerful story which begs the question, 'What would you do?'

IN A NUTSHELL: Sisterhood stretched to the limit.

'Two different faces, but in tight places, we think and we act as one.'

IRVING BERLIN, 'SISTERS'

My Sister, My Friend

'A loyal sister is worth a thousand friends.'

MARIAN EIGERMAN

Sisters are friends like no others. Who else would put up with quite so much? Who else knows your entire background? Who else knows exactly the right thing to say when times are tough?

THROUGH GOOD TIMES AND BAD

Sisters are there for you through thick and thin. Whether congratulating you on your new promotion or comforting you in the face of dismay or disappointment, a sister's support is second to none.

There's something about a sister's support that is very special. No matter what is troubling or exciting you, she's the one person you can rely on to share in your joy or pain.

UPS AND DOWNS

Sisters Kylie and Dannii Minogue have certainly had their fair share of ups and downs. When Kylie was diagnosed with breast cancer in 2005, Dannii rushed to Melbourne to be with her.

'I never thought she wouldn't make it. I couldn't. You don't,' a tearful Dannii told Piers Morgan later. 'All I wanted to do was get inside the door of the family home and see my gorgeous sister and hug her.'

Kylie successfully battled the disease and happier news, of Dannii's pregnancy, followed in January 2010, prompting a burst of excitement from 'Auntie' Kylie, who announced on Twitter, 'Congratulations to my sister Dannii on the happy news!!!! WOW WOW WOW!!'

FABULOUS PHONE CALLS

In the light of today's hectic lifestyles – when we all have so many commitments to honour, so many friends to see –

sometimes family takes a back seat when it comes to your social schedule.

But a sister is always available for a chat. If face-to-face time is just not possible, find an evening to call instead, curl up on the sofa and have a good old natter.

SPECIAL RELATIONSHIP

A sister is special because you can tell her things you might not tell anyone else – that are too personal for your parents, yet too embarrassing or private to share with your friends.

Whether confessing exactly how the rigours of labour made you feel, seeking help for a health concern, or facing up to a hard personal truth, a sister is sometimes the one person you can turn to.

'You can kid the world, but not your sister.'

CHARLOTTE GRAY

A SISTER IN NEED

Sisters are fantastic fun and wonderful shoulders to cry on – but they're also the best person to turn to when you're in need of some advice.

From being an agony aunt to running a twenty-four-hour chef helpline, sisters can proffer the right answer at the right time on any subject, even at the drop of a hat.

WARDROBE REVOLUTION

For example, every now and then, a girl has to admit her bulging wardrobe needs a clearout. When your closet is fit to burst and you still have nothing to wear, call in the cavalry. Get sis over to go through your outfits and help you decide which ones to throw.

How to Go About It

Split the decision into three piles – keep, chuck and swap – and ask her opinion if you're not sure. The swap pile will be all the items that you don't want, but your sister does.

Two sets of eyes are better than one in this situation and she may even suggest a way to customize or accessorize an item that changes your view of a former has-been.

She should also be honest enough to admit that she never liked the way an old favourite looked anyway, especially if you're insisting on clinging on to something that never once suited you.

If you still live together, you can do both wardrobes in one night. Otherwise, have two wardrobe nights – and another evening of girly fun.

ASK THE EXPERT

Sometimes, aptitude runs in the family. Perhaps your mum was green-fingered and you would spend hours in the garden with her, learning the trade of how to garden – you've probably both picked up a trick or two by adulthood.

But all sisters are different and all have different skills. Never be afraid to ask your sister for help if you're struggling in an area in which she succeeds – she'll be more than happy to oblige. After all, what else are sisters for?

SPREAD THE LOVE

And don't forget to offer your own expertise if you know she's finding a particular challenge tough. If she's a creative type and you're a maths whiz, suggest you help her with her tax return. If she's setting up a business and you're an IT genius, propose you design her company website.

Not only will you both be grateful for the extra help in the face of life's difficulties, but it will serve to strengthen the relationship you share.

> 'Helping one another is part of the religion of sisterhood.'
>
> LOUISA MAY ALCOTT

Sisters in the News

SISTERS 'MAKE PEOPLE HAPPY'

Yes, it's official! Researchers in this 2009 study, which quizzed 571 people aged seventeen to twenty-five about their lives, found that people who grew up with sisters were more likely to be happy and balanced.

The University of Ulster reported that sisters in a family made it 'more open and willing to discuss feelings'. In particular, they highlighted sisters' ability to help families heal after upsetting events such as divorce.

So the next time your sister makes you want to tear your hair out, remember that she's actually good for your mental health – believe it or not!

'Sisters appear to encourage more open communication and cohesion in families.'

PROFESSOR TONY CASSIDY

SYNCHRONICITY

Two sisters from Liverpool got the best Mother's Day present possible in March 2010 – they both gave birth the day before. Sisters Michelle Hunter and Donna Pooley went into labour hours apart, despite neither being due for weeks.

Michelle was first into Liverpool Women's Hospital, where 4lbs 10oz Astin arrived, while Donna later delivered baby Katlyn, who weighed in at 5lbs 3oz.

Staff at the hospital were equally surprised by the coincidence: 'I've been working here for nine years and have never known two sisters give birth on the same day,' said one.

Of course, there is an added bonus – neither sister will ever forget the birthday of their niece/nephew ...

BURNING LOVE

Jessica Lazaro didn't hesitate when she realized that her special-needs sister was inside a burning house – she ran straight in to save her.

The siblings had been celebrating Nicole's twenty-second birthday in the yard of their Sacramento home when the birthday girl went inside and somehow started a fire.

Soon smoke and flames were pouring from the house and Jessica realized her vulnerable sibling was missing. She rushed through their burning home and found Nicole in a bedroom, where she pushed her to safety through a window.

Firefighters said the act was 'heroic', but Jessica remarked, 'My first instinct was to go and get my sister – and that's what I did.'

THESE BOOTS WERE MADE FOR WALKING

Three sisters in Nepal made history – and headlines – by becoming trekking guides, which is typically an all-male pursuit in the region.

Though male porters and other trekkers used to gaze in astonishment at the sisters as they undertook their new career, the women have had the last laugh.

Lucky, Nikki and Dikki Chhetri set up Three Sisters Adventure Trekking, which guides tourists around precarious trails in the Himalayas, at the start of the millennium – and it's been a huge success. They are also training other Nepali women in the job.

Nikki said, 'They get inspired by us, how my sisters and I have built our business and an activist group for womens' rights.'

'How do people make it through life without a sister?'

SARA CORPENING

THE ULTIMATE GIFT

Having spent £30,000 on failed IVF treatments, Amanda Gudz thought she'd never be a mother. But then her little sister Sammy Lewin came to the rescue and proposed that she carry Amanda's child for her.

'I couldn't believe what I was hearing,' Amanda later said to the *Mirror*. 'Here was my little sister offering to make the biggest sacrifice.'

Sammy was implanted with two embryos in December 2007, conceived from Amanda's eggs and Amanda's husband's sperm. Nine months later, Amanda's daughter was born.

'I'll never forget the look on her face when she held Esme for the very first time,' revealed Sammy, who explained the surrogacy by saying, 'I see it like I've babysat Esme for nine months. You could say I was returning the favour to Mandy for babysitting me and my children over the years.'

'Bless you, my darling, and remember you are always in the heart – oh, tucked so close there is no chance of escape – of your sister.'

KATHERINE MANSFIELD

Holiday Time

In years gone by, you and your sibling would have been the best holiday buddies. Building sandcastles at the seaside, hanging up your stockings together on Christmas Eve, taking a stroll in the spring sunshine on a low-key city break ...

Some of your best childhood memories may come from those family vacations. A walk Mum and Dad dragged you on – to noisy discontent from both siblings – but that was amazing and unforgettable. The time the rain came into the tent, or the ants ate all the food. The summer you beat your older sibling at Scrabble (you haven't played since, so you're officially still the champ).

Keep the holiday spirit happening. As families grow, it can be difficult to get away all together, but there are plenty of villas on the continent to house your rowdy relatives, not to mention country cottages closer to home that would have enough beds for an extended brood.

> 'We acquire friends and we make enemies, but our sisters come with the territory.'
>
> EVELYN LOEB

SOAK UP SOME SUNSHINE

With air travel relatively cheap these days, what's to stop you and your sister sunning yourselves on a short break? If you're free and single, she'll be the perfect holiday partner. If you have families, a built-in babysitter (for both of you) will make the trip go even smoother.

Recline on a sun lounger and watch the world go by.

WEEKEND AWAY

If time is tight, why not opt for a weekend break instead? Getting away from it all could be more beneficial than you think.

You could plan the trip around a special family birthday – of your parents or siblings – so that the whole family is together to celebrate.

CAMP IT UP

Chances are those family holidays of your youth were camping trips – cheap, affordable, flexible accommodation that you will either have loved or hated.

Why not give it a whirl again? Take a road trip with your sibling: wherever you pitch your tent, that's your home.

SISTERS ARE DOING IT FOR THEMSELVES

Sometimes, a break just for you and your siblings, with no partners, parents or kids getting in the way, is a great idea.

You'll have opportunity to conduct long, intimate conversations, pursue selfishly the things the small group of you want to do, and make the most of the chance to reaffirm the close relationship you share.

You could even make it an annual event in the calendar.

MISTLETOE AND WINE

Inevitably, as Christmas comes around, so too does a stay with family. For most people, this is a joyous opportunity to cement traditions and share time with one another at a special moment of the year.

It is also, however, notoriously stressful, as people pull out all the stops to have fantastic family fun. Perhaps the following ideas will oil the wheels of the festive locomotion ...

'In the cookies of life, sisters are the chocolate chips.'

AUTHOR UNKNOWN

TOO MANY COOKS?

They may spoil the broth, but sometimes a helping hand in the kitchen is exactly what is required. If your sibling is hosting Christmas, offer to bring a dish for Christmas Eve with you, to save them having to rustle up at least one gourmet meal.

Or you could offer to make the mince pies or the Christmas pud – just something to share the strain.

If time allows, why not jointly make some of the essential Christmas offerings? A session in the kitchen together will be fun as well as productive.

SWEET SHAPES

These peppermint-flavoured treats are great to make for the festive season, providing a break from heavier fare but still satisfying a sister's sweet tooth.

It's a kid-friendly recipe, too, so you could get the whole family involved in making them.

Makes 35

INGREDIENTS

1 egg white
350g (12oz) icing sugar
A few drops of peppermint oil
Decorations (optional)

METHOD

① Set a small amount of sugar to one side (enough to sprinkle beneath your rolled-out mixture, like flour when rolling pastry).

② Whisk the egg white in a large bowl until it foams.

③ Gradually sift in half the sugar and mix well until the concoction becomes creamy. Keep slowly adding the rest of the sugar, combining thoroughly after each addition, until the mixture is stiff and smooth. As it thickens, you may prefer to use your hands for the mixing, rather than an implement or electric whisk.

④ Add the peppermint oil.

⑤ Sprinkle the sugar you had set aside on to a table and roll out the mixture (a thickness of 4–5 mm should be ample). Using festive cutters, cut out stars, Christmas trees, reindeers and other shapes.

⑥ Decorate if desired – using melted chocolate, silver balls, or other decorations of your choice.

⑦ Place the shapes on a sheet of greaseproof paper and leave to dry out for 24 hours, then store in an airtight container.

⑧ Serve as an after-dinner alternative treat to chocolates.

SHOP TILL YOU DROP

The Christmas shopping frenzy is always a mass of lists and frantic phone calls, such as to check if nephew Danny would like Toy X instead of Toy Y, as the latter has been sold out since September.

Why not share your pain with your sister and book in a day to embark on the shopping together? It might not make it any less fraught, but at least you'll be stoically suffering through it together.

WHO GOES WHERE?

As families grow larger, commitments to family soon rack up. As sisters marry, have children and extend their immediate family, it's inevitable that it may not always be possible to spend the big day all together – the 'other side' of the family want attention and family time too.

Accept this early on and learn to compromise. Perhaps alternate where you spend Christmas each year so that everyone gets the opportunity to celebrate together.

Always try, however, to have at least one meal with your siblings around this special time of year to mark the event. The act of sharing food, drinking wine and toasting each other's health is a beautiful bonding experience you won't want to miss.

> 'A sister shares childhood memories and grown-up dreams.'
>
> AUTHOR UNKNOWN

Ladies of Letters

As in the fields of music and entertainment, the world of literature has produced some fantastically successful siblings who have pursued – to joint acclaim – the same ambition.

Here are a handful of the most celebrated.

THE BRONTË SISTERS

Charlotte, Emily and Anne all produced their first novel in the same year, 1847, and took the world of literature by storm. Raised in Haworth, North Yorkshire, where their father was a curate, they had two older sisters, Maria and Elizabeth, and a brother, Branwell, who became an artist and poet.

Unusually for girls at the time, Charlotte and Emily, along with the two older sisters, were sent to school in 1824, but they were recalled after Maria and Elizabeth contracted tuberculosis there and later died.

Writers from a young age, in 1846 the sisters self-published a book of poems under the names Currer, Ellis and Acton Bell (their pseudonyms designed to be androgynous in the sexist world of publishing), but it attracted little interest.

The following year, their debut novels, published in a three-volume set – comprising of Charlotte's *Jane Eyre*, Emily's

Wuthering Heights and Anne's *Agnes Grey* – were published to critical acclaim.

The sisters set about writing more, but tragedy was to strike the family time and time again, cutting short their promising literary careers.

Emily died a year after her romantic novel, set on the Yorskhire moors that surrounded their home, was published, having caught a cold at their brother's funeral. She was thirty.

Anne managed to produce a second novel, *The Tenant of Wildfell Hall* (1848), before succumbing to consumption at the age of twenty-nine.

Charlotte saw *Shirley* (1849) and *Villette* (1853) published before her marriage, in 1854, to curate Arthur Bell Nicholls. Pregnant with their first child, she died a year later, possibly from tuberculosis or from dehydration caused by extreme morning sickness.

The tragic yet productive lives of the Brontë sisters not only left behind a legacy of fine literature, but also opened the door to other female writers; Anne and Charlotte revealed their true identities to their publisher shortly before Anne's death.

The enormous success of *Jane Eyre* eventually led to Charlotte joining the London literary set and encouraging a feminist movement in writers.

MARGARET DRABBLE AND A. S. BYATT

Born in Sheffield in 1936 and 1939 respectively, sisters A. S. (Antonia) Byatt and Margaret Drabble have become two of Britain's most celebrated and critically acclaimed authors.

Although younger, Margaret beat her sister to the first novel, publishing *The Summer Bird-Cage* in 1963, a year before A. S. Byatt's *The Shadow of the Sun*.

In total, Margaret has written seventeen novels, as well as short stories and plays, while Antonia boasts nine novels, plus several volumes of short stories, essays and academic texts. In 1990, she won the Booker Prize for her novel *Possession*.

However, Margaret beat her big sister once again when it came to the Queen's honours list. She was made a Dame in 1980, ten whole years before the same honour was bestowed on Antonia.

Byatt's second novel, *The Game* (1967), is a study of the relationship between two sisters.

JOAN AND JACKIE COLLINS

Although Joan Collins is best known as an actress – most notably in the role of Alexis Colby in the 1980s hit TV show *Dynasty* – of late she has also moved into writing novels like her sister Jackie, as well as penning a beauty guide.

'I'm older than my sister so I started writing first,' said Joan in one interview. 'I started writing at school. I was always top of my class in composition, essays, English Lit and all of that.'

She still has some way to go to beat her sister's record, though: Jackie has notched up twenty-six bestselling blockbusters over the course of her publishing career.

'A sister can be seen as someone who is both ourselves and very much not ourselves – a special kind of double.'

TONI MORRISON

Days Out

Whether you are in your teens or entering the 'golden age', a day out with your sister is the perfect way to bond and unwind from the stress of modern living.

Shopping trips, cinema nights and dinner dates are ideal ways to meet up on a regular basis, but how about surprising her with something a little different?

A NEW LOOK

No matter what age you are, you are probably applying the same make-up you have used for years and very few of us have ever had professional tips. Time for a radical makeover?

GRAB A FREEBIE

Most make-up counters in department stores and leading chemists offer a full makeover, which won't cost you a penny, although one or two charge a nominal fee.

Make sure you book in advance, so you won't be disappointed, and, if possible, try to find a counter with two make-up artists so you can be beautified simultaneously. There is no obligation to buy the products, but you may feel you want to, so be prepared.

TAKE TIME OUT

Do a little research into the kind of make-up you and your sister would best suit – e.g. young and funky or a more sophisticated look – and allow a good 45 minutes for your transformation.

It may seem a long time to schedule into your busy lives, but it's a great experience to share with a sister and there's something incredibly relaxing about sitting in a chair, being preened and pampered and knowing you can't move for a while.

MAKE A DAY OF IT

As the stores are invariably located in towns or shopping centres, you can make a day of it by treating yourself – and your new faces – to a nice lunch or a spot of window-shopping, just to make sure you are seen in public.

MILK AND TWO SUGARS

Spoil yourselves by booking a slot for afternoon tea at a posh hotel or tea room. A pot of Earl Grey, cucumber sandwiches and scones with jam and cream will always be just the ticket.

If budgets don't stretch to something flash, why not take it in turns to host tea at each other's houses? A cake doesn't cost much to bake, but it will certainly make for some delicious afternoons.

If you are splashing out, have a glass of champers to go with your tea. It will add a little fizz to proceedings!

MONKEYING AROUND

When was the last time you climbed a tree?

Swinging about in the woods is all the rage these days; there is guaranteed to be a centre near you where you can get in touch with your inner ape. All over the country, aerial adventure schemes are taking people up to the treetops for a fun-packed day of zip wires, rope bridges and climbing.

Although not recommended if you have a fear of heights, it's all regulated and safe, and you will be wearing a harness. Admittedly, it's not cheap, but it guarantees a day that you and your sister will never forget.

> 'A sibling may be the keeper of one's identity, the only person with the keys to one's unfettered, more fundamental self.'
>
> MARIAN SANDMAIER

For a slightly less expensive option, you could hark back to your rock-climbing days with an hour on a climbing wall. They can be found in many leisure centres as well as some shopping centres, and make a brilliant activity for all ages.

Again, you will be wearing a harness – so you are in no danger of breaking any bones.

RETRO PICNIC

Remember those endless summer days, lazing in the park or on a riverbank, running round with your siblings and eating jam sandwiches?

Everyone has happy memories of a family picnic and siblings will share the same ones, so what better way to promote a feeling of indulgent nostalgia than by recreating a favourite childhood day?

CHOOSING THE PERFECT PICNIC SPOT

If you still live in the area, you could choose a favourite spot that you enjoyed as children, or travel further afield to one you might have visited on a special occasion.

PICKING YOUR PICNIC

Try to remember all the treats your parents put in the picnic basket and recreate them. Packaging them the same is half the fun. For example, if sandwiches always came in tinfoil, wrap yours up too. If there were always real plates and cutlery, restage the scene.

Here are a few ideas for food, which many will remember from childhood – but you may well have some family favourites of your own.

- Boiled new potatoes or potato salad
- Coleslaw
- Hard-boiled eggs, still in their shells
- Pork pies
- Melon slices
- Jam sandwiches
- Ham sandwiches
- Malt loaf slices
- Jamaican ginger cake
- Iced buns
- Orange or lemon barley water

How about some traditional rock cakes to round off the feast?

ROCK CAKES

Makes 12

INGREDIENTS

225g (8oz) self-raising flour
110g (4oz) butter or margarine
110g (4oz) caster sugar
½ teaspoon of finely grated orange or lemon rind
150g (5oz) sultanas (or mixed dried fruit)
1 large or 2 small eggs
25ml milk
A little water
Demerara sugar for sprinkling (optional)

METHOD

① Pre-heat the oven to Gas Mark 6/200°C/425°F.

② Sieve the flour into a large mixing bowl and add the butter or margarine in small dollops. Rub the flour and fat together until they resemble breadcrumbs.

③ Add the sugar, lemon rind and dried fruit and mix well.

④ Add the egg and stir in.

⑤ Gradually mix in the milk and a little of the water until the consistency is doughy.

⑥ Grease a baking tray and plop even-sized dollops of dough on to it, well spaced to allow the buns to spread (use a second baking tray if necessary).

⑦ Sprinkle with demerara sugar (if using), then bake for 12–15 minutes.

⑧ Cool on a wire rack.

OPTIONAL EXTRAS

Don't forget the following to add to the fun:

- Camera
- Beach ball
- Football
- Frisbee
- Skipping rope
- Bubble mixture

Cool bags and chests are all the rage, but if you are not travelling too far or staying out too long before lunch, a traditional picnic basket is much nicer, provided you can get hold of one.

You can still keep things cool by putting an ice pack and the most perishable foods inside a plastic bag.

FAMILY GAMES

Continuing the nostalgia theme, everyone remembers their mum and dad setting up family contests and encouraging all relatives to take part. Whether it's a card game, a race to the shoreline or a full-on game of footie, family games mean

laughter, happiness and, okay, perhaps a little competitive spirit. But that's 'character-building', isn't it?

Why not spend a family day out reviving some of the games you used to play together in your youth? Let your inner child have the time of her life!

BUTTERFINGERS

As simple as a game can get, but still great fun. This can be played with any number of people, even just the two of you, and all you need is a ball.

- Stand a few metres apart, facing each other (if there are two people) or in a circle.
- Throw the ball between you and if anyone drops it, they must go down on one knee.
- Another drop means two knees; then an arm behind the back; then both arms behind the back!
- The disadvantaged player must catch the ball three times in a row to lose each handicap.
- If there are more than two players, throw the ball to other people in random order and fool them with dummy throws, before aiming at someone else.

> 'We get along really well, but TV and film aren't reality. We're best friends, but we do have our fights!'
>
> MARY-KATE OLSEN

'Having a sister is like having a best friend you can't get rid of. You know whatever you do, they'll still be there.'

AMY LI

PICNIC OLYMPICS

Here's your opportunity to wreak revenge for all the times your sibling beat you at school sports day! Pick as many traditional, but silly, events as you like and compete for the gold medal. Games can be played by two or more.

Events could include:

- Limbo contests, using a fallen branch, a piece of string or a skipping rope.
- Egg and spoon race.
- A dressing-up race (coats, shoes, cardigans, and so on, are dotted at intervals and have to be put on as you run).
- Sack race (you'll need a couple of large, strong plastic bags for this one).
- Three-legged race (if there are four or more people).
- Obstacle race (use lunch boxes, skipping ropes and so on to provide the obstacles).

If you have enough equipment for all the events, you can compete at the same time. If not, use a watch or stopwatch (found on most mobile phones) to time each event.

GAMING ACTIVITIES

If ball games and informal fun in the great outdoors aren't really your sister's thing, you could always take the contest to somewhere a little more 'civilized', and try a more organized outing. How about one of the following?

- Bowling
- Pitch and putt
- Quasar (laser gun shoot-out)
- Ice skating or roller skating
- A game of pool

> 'I, who have no sisters or brothers, look with some degree of innocent envy on those who may be said to be born to friends.'
>
> JAMES BOSWELL

Record-Breakers

These remarkable siblings have all entered the worldwide record books.

RIPE OLD AGE

The Thornton sisters were local celebrities in Louisiana, USA. Maggie Rae Thornton Renfro was the fourth oldest person in the world and the oldest African-American on her death at 114, while Carrie Lee made 107 and Rosie Lee lived until 103.

On 8 November 2009, the sisters were recognized in a ceremony hosted by Cultural Crossroads at the Minden Civic Center in Louisiana. At the time, they had the oldest combined age of three living siblings at 324 years.

MIRACLE GIRLS

Lithuanian conjoined twins Vilija and Vatalija Tamulevicius were born on 30 March 1987, sharing a skull and a cranial circulatory system, a condition known as a Craniopagus connection. All previous efforts to separate Craniopagus twins had resulted in death or brain damage to one or both babies, so the prognosis was not good.

Russian specialist Dr Alexander Konovalov operated to separate the girls on 6 July 1989, but their bodies rejected the artificial skulls. The girls were then flown to Dallas, Texas, where American doctor Kenneth E. Salyer rebuilt their skulls.

Following the successful operations, the miracle babies returned home to Lithuania with no brain damage – and both survived.

SPEEDY SISTERS

The moment that Tirunesh Dibaba became the most successful athlete in the history of the World Cross-Country Championships, winning a fifth international gold medal in 2008, she had one thing on her mind – her little sister.

Just an hour beforehand, seventeen-year-old Genzebe Dibaba had become the surprise winner of the junior women's gold. The amazing dual feat made them the first family members to win gold medals at the competition.

And these two aren't the only athletes in the family: older sister Ejegayehu was in the winning team at the 2004 World Championships and won a silver at the Athens Olympics, and brother Dejene is now making his mark on international athletics too.

'Yes, I am very happy to win again, but I am more happy about my sister than I am about myself.'

TIRUNESH DIBABA

LOVE ADVANTAGE

'I always like to win, but I'm the big sister. I want to make sure she has everything, even if I don't have anything.'

VENUS WILLIAMS

Just a year apart in age and a whisper apart in sporting ability, tennis aces Venus and Serena Williams take sibling rivalry to a new level. Having faced each other twenty-three times in professional matches, including eight Grand Slam finals, Serena has emerged the victor, claiming thirteen wins and six Grand Slam titles from her older sister.

Both of them have hit the international record books, though – at the US Open, Venus is ranked fourth in the category of most matches won in succession, unbeaten in twenty matches between 2000 and 2002; Serena, meanwhile, is the youngest

ever mixed doubles champion at Wimbledon: she was sixteen years and 282 days old when she won in 1998.

Together, they have also had considerable success in the Grand Slam doubles, scooping the Wimbledon trophy four times by 2009.

'Family's first, and that's what matters most. We realize that our love goes deeper than the tennis game. Tennis is just a game, family is forever.'

SERENA WILLIAMS

BOLLYWOOD VOICES

Lata Mangeshkar and Asha Bhosle are Bollywood's leading singers. They began to sing on movie soundtracks, as well as act, aged thirteen and nine, in order to support their family after their father's death.

The girls carved out successful careers for themselves, with Lata initially being the most lauded, often landing the songs of the heroines, while Asha sang the less prestigious parts of the bad girls and temptresses. Between 1974 and 1991, Lata was named in the *Guinness Book of World Records* as the record-holder for the most recordings in the world, estimated at 30,000 tracks.

However, some dispute of the veracity of this claim and others, including Asha herself, claim that the younger sister is the record-holder with a total of over 12,000 recordings to her name.

SAFETY IN NUMBERS

In December 1998, Nkem Chukwu made history when she gave birth to six girls and two boys in a Houston hospital. They were the first set of octuplets to be born alive.

Eduka, the eldest, arrived on 15 December, and her seven siblings followed twelve days later. Sadly, one of the girls died a week after the birth, but the seven surviving children have grown up to be happy and healthy.

The children's parents had used fertility treatment before having the octuplets, but, four years later, they were naturally blessed with another girl; they named her Divine Favour.

The Chukwu octuplets, as they are known in the US, live in a six-bedroom house in Houston, Texas, and are driven around in a 16-seater minibus.

Although the Chukwu children were the first octuplets to be live born, the record for the longest surviving octuplets is now held by the children of single mum Nadia Suleman, whose unorthodox IVF treatment caused controversy and resulted in eight surviving babies in 2009.

TWIN TIMES

There's nothing unusual in the fact that Keilani Marie Cardago shares a birthday with her twin sister. But she also shares it with little sisters Mikayla Anee and Malia Abigail, also twins. The older girls were born on 30 May 1996 and their siblings on the same date seven years later.

This is not the only case of twins who share birthdays with twins in the same family, though:

- American mother Laura Shelley gave birth to Melissa Nicole and Mark Fredrick Julian Junior in 1990 and Kayla May and Jonathan Price Moore in 2003, both on 25 March.
- Michele Gorney, also in the US, gave birth to her children on 18 March: Kaitlin Mary Garcia and Morgan Mary Garcia in 1996, and Reece Shae Rushton and Riley Sy Rushton in 2006.

'One of the best things about being an adult is the realization that you can share with your sister and still have plenty for yourself.'

BETSY COHE

Great Gifts

> 'A sister is a gift to the heart, a friend to the spirit, a golden thread to the meaning of life.'
>
> ISADORA JAMES

No matter how well you know your sibling, you may struggle to find that perfect present when it comes to Christmas and birthdays.

This section contains a few ideas to help you choose something more original or meaningful than the usual hurriedly wrapped offerings.

PAST AND PRESENT

Enlist the help of Mum or Dad and produce a 'memory box'. Here's how:

- Buy or decorate a container, about the size of a shoebox, and fill it with little mementoes of your sibling's life.
- If possible, have a rummage in your parents' loft – you'll be amazed what you discover. There may be a tiny pair of baby shoes, or a lock of baby hair, kept by Mum all those years ago. Or you could come across the first single she ever bought, a book she won as a school prize, or some early artwork she daubed.
- Add a few funny photos and write down a memory or two from the family history.

Make sure you are there when she opens it, so you can share a laugh at the memories.

A BARREL OF LAUGHS

If you can't be with your sister as often as you'd like, let her know you are thinking of her every day with this unique gift.

Fill a pretty jar, or barrel, with 365 thoughts, jokes and sayings that sum up your relationship, make you laugh or just ring true about your lives. There are a few dotted throughout this book, but here are a couple more:

'Sisters annoy, interfere, criticize. Indulge in monumental sulks, in huffs, in snide remarks. Borrow. Break. Monopolize the bathroom. Are always underfoot. But if catastrophe should strike, sisters are there. Defending you against all comers.'
Pam Brown

'We are sisters. We will always be sisters. Our differences may never go away, but neither, for me, will our song.'
Elizabeth Fishel

PICTURE PERFECT

Had a family holiday or a weekend away together in recent years? If you have a great collection of snaps either on your computer or tucked away in a drawer somewhere, share them with your sibling.

There are now very reasonably priced offers for personalized photo albums (which look like glossy books), and the more you order, the cheaper they get – so you can stock up for other members of the family too.

'A sister smiles when one tells one's stories – for she knows where the decoration has been added.'
CHRIS MONTAIGNE

Here are some other ideas of gifts you could make with your family photos.

- Why not turn your pictures into a fabulous calendar, which means your sister will get a reminder of the good times you spent together every day?
- Perhaps you have a favourite picture of the two of you that you can turn into a fun gift, like a mousemat or a mug.
- Alternatively, you could buy an ordinary photo album and fill it with photos and memories yourself. Don't forget the witty captions!

MESSAGE BRACELET

A beautiful piece of jewellery with a personal message will ensure your sister can carry your sentiments with her wherever she goes. You can get mail-order message bracelets or order online but, better still, first choose a piece of jewellery you know she would love and then have it engraved.

Flat bracelets could have the message engraved inside; some chain bracelets come with a flat disc attached for a short engraving.

Top Tip: Don't choose anything too embarrassingly gushy for your message, but use a nickname or a familiar phrase that expresses your affection instead.

'Sisters share the scent and smells – the feel of a common childhood.'

PAM BROWN

FAMILY CONNECTION

You share a family, so why not find out more about your family tree and present her with the result?

This one will take a little time, but it will be a standing testament to your shared history and will be passed on to your own kids.

WHERE TO BEGIN?

Start with your oldest living relatives and pump them for as much information as they can muster. Names, dates of birth, occupations and where they lived are all great launching pads for a search.

TV programmes tracing ancestors, plus the online publication of documents such as the 1911 Census, have fuelled a growing interest in personal history, and there are now many websites that will help you, too.

If you think your sibling would enjoy taking the journey with you, sign both of you up to an ancestral tracing site as a gift. Then you have the added bonus of spending more time together and achieving a joint goal.

LET YOUR TREE TAKE ROOT

Find out as many stories as you can about your relatives and then present them in a book, with your family tree at the front.

Remember that the dry facts of your genealogy are just the start. The more colourful anecdotes you can include, the better!

'Our roots say we're sisters, our hearts say we're friends.'

AUTHOR UNKNOWN

Also available in this bestselling series:

The Boys' Book	ISBN 978-1-905158-64-5	Price: £7.99
The Girls' Book	ISBN 978-1-905158-79-9	Price: £7.99
The Mums' Book	ISBN 978-1-84317-246-8	Price: £9.99
The Dads' Book	ISBN 978-1-84317-250-5	Price: £9.99
The Grannies' Book	ISBN 978-1-84317-251-2	Price: £9.99
The Grandads' Book	ISBN 978-1-84317-308-3	Price: £9.99
The Aunts' Book	ISBN 978-1-84317-459-2	Price: £9.99
The Wives' Book	ISBN 978-1-84317-325-0	Price: £9.99
The Husbands' Book	ISBN 978-1-84317-326-7	Price: £9.99
The Lovers' Book	ISBN 978-1-84317-285-7	Price: £9.99
The Friends' Book	ISBN 978-1-84317-359-5	Price: £9.99
The Cooks' Book	ISBN 978-1-84317-328-1	Price: £9.99
The Gardeners' Book	ISBN 978-1-84317-327-4	Price: £9.99
The Christmas Book	ISBN 978-1-84317-282-6	Price: £9.99
The Family Book	ISBN 978-1-906082-10-9	Price: £14.99

These titles and all other Michael O'Mara books
are available by post from:

Bookpost Ltd
PO Box 29, Douglas, Isle of Man IM99 1BQ

To pay by credit card, please use the following contact details:

Telephone: 01624 677237 / Fax: 01624 670923

Email: bookshop@enterprise.net

Internet: www.bookpost.co.uk

Postage and packing is free in the UK; overseas customers
allow £5 per hardback book.